If you wish to book a talk or introductory
synergy light group sessions in your area you
are welcome to contact the author.

Please e-mail Jackie at jackiequeally@gmail.com

For William Buehler and all those committed to the
process of Ascension

The Spiritual Purpose of Rosslyn: Key to a Hidden Matrix

Published by the author

ISBN
978-0-9541435-5-8

List of Contents

Figure 1: The Female Half of the Reshel Showing Basic Poles
Figure 2: The Upper and Lower Halves of the Reshel
Figure 3: The Upper and Lower halves of the Reshel with Basic Poles Superimposed on
Rosslyn Chapel
Figure 4: The Principle Modes of Reality
Figure 5: Golden Ratio Rhombus showing the "L" in its centre-right upright position
Figure 6: Two Golden Ratio Rhombuses showing the New Resh point where they intersect at "A"
Figure 7: Golden Ratio Rhombuses and the "L" with Rosslyn at the Resh point where they Intersect
Figure 8: The Rose Line Passing through Edinburgh grid showing Poles of the Basic Reshel
Figure 9: The Sinclair Cross
Figure 10: The Resh within the Christic half of the Golden

Chapter 2: Rosslyn and the Reshel

Foreword with Note of Thanks

Architecture follows function. If the function is Ascension or related dynamics, such as the Reshel, then architecture will use the geometry and alchemy to enhance the function.
William Buehler 2007

This guide focuses on Rosslyn Chapel and its locality, as an area of exceptional spiritual activity and purpose. The content and graphics refer to a highly evolved spiritual system at play in Rosslyn Chapel, which have been detailed by my friend and colleague William Buehler. These spiritual systems derive from an esoteric body of knowledge that Buehler and Light beings in the inner dimensions call the "Reshel", of interest to those seriously studying esoteric knowledge. ("Reshel" in Hebrew means "Chief Headstone of God"). The Reshel system manifests in a dynamic matrix of ley lines in the area as well as within the intricately woven design of Rosslyn Chapel. The guide introduces the basic concepts of sacred (Reshel) geometry together with the ancient yet still pertinent cosmology concurrent with the Reshel, applying that knowledge to geomancy/the study of earth energies and consciousness often found in grids and ley lines. The ley lines that abound in and around Rosslyn Chapel align with Reshel formats that were utilised over the millennia at Rosslyn and are active now.

William Buehler is an American citizen who retired in 1976 as a Naval Commander in the US Navy in order to dedicate the rest of his life to esoteric research into what is today broadly called Ascension Dynamics. Buehler's work is based on the proto-Sinaitic method of drawing letters that he was divinely guided to in the Jewish Encyclopedia at American University, Washington DC. He discovered that these glyphs and geometric implications were apparently used by Templars and Masons in early times. His overview of the types of earth grids in existence today can be found in **Appendix C**. From this succinct list we can see that the Reshel is a specialised system of man-made leys, combined with natural aspects that offer a very powerful tool for organising, orchestrating and adapting to earth and cosmic energies in co-operation with mentors on the inner planes of reality.

He shares and develops his research with others on the basis of a totally free global interchange of knowledge. Gifted with an exceptional mind, many regard him as one of the world's foremost geomancers and mystics as well as the leading authority on the Reshel. (The sheer volume of synchronicities and instant manifestations in relation to the Reshel that have occurred in my life convince me of the high level of accuracy of his knowledge and wisdom.) He corresponds extensively regarding Rosslyn and many other sites and sacred earth grid systems that the Reshel encompasses in its ever expanding system.

The word "Reshel" is based on the Hebrew letter Resh meaning Chief Headstone of God. Buehler is a highly creative student of the earliest form of Hebrew letters, and from his studies he has developed a body of knowledge that many perceive as ingenious. He believes the letters were designed as an energetic system of "light codes" for consciousness-raising and enlightenment and they contain Reshel dynamics in their codes. Translations of the Jewish Scriptures and Bible from the original Hebrew are quite misleading since they obscure these codes. From a metaphysical point of view the meaning changes and is lost quite dramatically when translating proto- Sinaitic glyphs into modern languages that are not consciously encoded with spiritual vibrations. The Biblical references used in this book are based on interpretation using the Reshel.

I have written a companion volume entitled **"The Spiritual Meaning of Rosslyn's Carvings"** that is concerned with how the details of the carvings in Rosslyn Chapel reflect the language of the Reshel and mirror a series of initiations connected to the timeless mysteries of creation. In both these volumes I attempt to simplify some of the main ideas William has put forward at this critical time in our history. In my attempt to communicate these ideas with simplicity I only ask that you will feel in your hearts whether this resonates with you as you read. In addition to William Buehler's ideas I include some of my own research and perceptions and also valuable information freely given to me by friends, colleagues and specialists in various fields whom I have met as clients.

The Reshel study tours

Since a young age I have felt that the earth is a sentient being that relates to and affects human consciousness in a subtle way. In 1999 I began to operate day tours to ancient sites that I discovered close to Edinburgh. Many of the sites were rather hidden off the beaten track…places that bore a certain charm and were often associated with old legends. Legends can testify to the sacred energies of the earth and sky, as the legends were born in a time when the culture was more sensitive to these things. Long before I began conducting tours in 1999 I was aware of the special quality that Rosslyn held but was unaware of its significance to the Reshel. The Reshel embodies the complex dynamics of creation, reflected in evolving etheric geometric patterns that anchor themselves in the earth's physical plane at key sites. It turned out that many of the ancient and natural sites I had chosen for my tours were on key nodes within the Reshel pattern of grids. Not only were my tour itineraries following the lines without my consciously knowing of it at that point, but I discovered that many other places on a more global level that I had lived in or visited earlier in my life happened to be key nodes in the Reshel grids of the Earth. From the start I included Rosslyn Chapel in the tours, and later realised that the site interconnects both historically and "energetically" (through the ley lines and geometric alignments) with many other sites. This includes the history of families such as the Sinclairs of Rosslyn whose involvement in outward events bear spiritual witness to the hidden codes of the Reshel.

I have been fortunate to have corresponded with William Buehler since at least 1997, and when I began posing the question to various geomancers and geometers: "What is the purpose of these ley lines that seem to so fascinate the technically-minded men who map them out?" I found William was the only person who could answer this adequately for my purposes. As he shared his understanding of ley lines of the Reshel with me, I began to realise that I had a particularly strong affinity with them. Drawing from his profound and prolonged study of the Reshel, William provided me with answers that in my mind supply the most satisfactory, detailed and deep explanation of ley lines and other esoteric phenomena. For many, the sheer technicality of the grids presented is baffling and they withdraw their interest, but for those who can attune to them in whichever way they resonate, the patterns begin to speak to them alchemically it seems.

Even after eight years or so of running the tours, sites I chose are revealing fresh evidence of their "telluric" properties (hot spots in terms of earth energies); as new Reshel patterns in the locality emerge. The Reshel is dynamically linked to universal consciousness or sentience, and as it shifts new patterns will emerge, particularly so in these times of immense evolutionary change and growth. As I began to realise the significance of how the Reshel system of energies engages at a deep level with the mysteries of the cosmos, I met William Buehler face-to-face and was invited to study with him.

I am indebted to him for transforming my modest tourist enterprise into a very deep spiritual endeavour that borders on what many see as a way of life.

In return many people feel that their paths have been deepened after visiting Rosslyn and other sites with me. I would say that this is a matter of what occurs when exposed to the sites in a sensitive fashion. The energy of the sites interacts with Spirit through me (due to my long time here being involved in the areas' essential mysteries and because the Reshel is a universal mystical language that threads its way through the sites once you begin to tune into them). I tend to "tune in" to people so as to communicate better and enable them to feel the energies at levels which suit their individual soul capacities. Often standing quietly for just a few minutes is all it takes for this to occur. It is not something that requires a great deal of planning, but it helps to be open and prepared inwardly for consciousness to shift in subtle ways, to notice when it does and then to discern the reason for it occurring at that time.

I run intensive Reshel study tours based in Roslin and elsewhere, and these last from two to five days. People learn the basic skills of participating in a Reshel light group and then the group links energetically to the ley lines that are currently most active.
I am planning tours of the large Pentagon over Southern Norway found by Harald Boehlke, Templar trails of Scotland and earth grid tours of the Rennes Le Chateau region of France in the near future since they energetically key into Rosslyn; details provided in **Appendix A**.

I would like to thank Andrew Gilmour for his painstaking patience in helping with editing and drawing all the figures in the book; also of course William Buehler for his prompt and expert checking of details appertaining to the Reshel. Thanks to Rab Wilkie for his insights, Ian Dinwiddie for checking grammar and providing quiet support as a good friend, Carol Mann for her early stage encouragement and Nicola Moss for all the hours of light work we shared before she moved away from Scotland. Also many thanks to Ruth my daughter for designing the cover while moving jobs and home, the lovely ground staff at Rosslyn

Chapel for their kind efforts and wishes in selling my sister book over the past year, and Iain Cormack the printer who always seemed to have my best interests at heart.

Finally, I hope you enjoy this book that I have been holding in seed form for many years.

Acknowledgement

When seeking further details, verification and identification of the energies in the Reshel, Buehler has consulted with Rev Maia Nartoomid since the early 1970s. She is a highly experienced conscious channel for Thoth/ Hermes who has been her primary spiritual "benefactor" since 1977. According to Maia/ Thoth, the Earth is under the mandate of Archangel Michael who is overseen by the highest archangel available to us; Metatron and a Seraphic order "The Ennead". Whenever Thoth is mentioned in the book it is Maia's gifted communication that has brought this forth.   I have at times simplified Maia Nartoomid's explanations which does not imply that the Nartoomids or Thoth agree with either my own or Beuhler's applications of their information. Her contact details are provided in **Appendix B,** in conjunction with William Buehler's e-mail address.

Chapter One: The Reshel

Cosmology

All of what follows appertains to higher worlds than our own in which spiritual realities eventually mould our own reality. Spiritual law dictates that there first is a foundation of Silence (Life) and Grace preceding the thought form/ vibration / geometric form / light pattern. These forms gradually trickle down to our denser world and become our daily reality – the true potential of many of the light forms is never realised due to the freedom of will at the human interface, and a variety of shortfalls in non-physical realms too. Humans are not yet fully aware of the power of their own thoughts and how they can interface with the divine for common good. Post-modern culture has become uniformly devoid of higher realities and as a consequence of spiritual worlds not being acknowledged, many people sense the absence of spiritual interpretations in our secular society, and are seeking in their own ways to connect with other dimensions to life. The Reshel provides a safe interface with such worlds, when used in company with the higher agencies in the inner planes.

The Earth was once within a time wave that was of a higher reality, where there was no separation between the divine and human other than that of their natural realms of being. There was a tear in the fabric of that time-space when karmic forces built up to a point where the Earth could no longer keep on its original track. In effect the tear separated the Earth reality from the greater reality that Thoth calls the *"Ranna Time Flow"* (terms in italics can be found in the Glossary) or *"Ranna Wave"*. Many cultures refer to this separation as a legendary Fall. This fall created a gap called the Kali Rift, which lies between the *Ranna* true time flow and our present time continuum, where Earth currently resides within an Oritronic (half light) reality. However, she is rapidly transiting this state to return home to the original Metatronic state she abided in. In order to assist the Earth in her mission, past guardians of the earth exercised their deep intent to heal the Earth of the rift that occurred and to proceed with the original objectives. Over many time periods the priests created ley line systems in co-operation with more divine sentient beings, and their intent was to allow the lines to connect with all levels of sentience (elementals, angels, humans etc), and thus subtly interact with the evolution of human consciousness. The priests and priestesses of ancient times were empathetic to the Earth, and studied how to align with Her in deep honour of her being and destiny. They knew that the Earth had to be restored to a higher harmony that had escaped her ever since the legendary fall common to many ancient myths. The Earth had fallen into a different and lower frequency – in other words Earth had fallen from its Metatronic frequencies of a full light spectrum to the lower Oritronic spectrum of half light frequencies.

The Kali Rift is the earth's micro-version of the Universal Tear that occurs in a wider galactic area. During this Fall Lucifer and the Nephilim (fallen angels) induced a field of evil intent that lent humanity a steep learning curve and also actually serves to disrupting the return journey. In a higher reality where time is more real, the past, future and present time continua all exist simultaneously and no such evil intent exists. In the Metatronic reality all fallen angels are redeemed. From a historical or linear viewpoint Earth was aligned with the *Ranna* Time Flow in the past, and will return to it in the future. This return process has now begun.

Since the process between man and nature is not a one–way flow, the thoughts and actions of each individual bear responsibility for the outcome of this deep etheric process within the Earth and cosmos. The lessons of this last zodiacal age were to achieve individual illumination and relevant dharmic service. Now this Self focus shifts to much the same in Group focussed service. Self illumination is assumed at this point. (Whether the soul exercises that skill to the level required is a matter of Free Will and initiative.)

To summarize, the Reshel is the main Metatronic system used to orchestrate Universal (re)evolution "back" into the Metatronic *Ranna* Time Wave of all the real universes and to accomplish the original objective of creating a new quality of Human race. When this occurs we will have shifted completely from a position of fear-based thoughts with its negative overtones into a new wavelength borne of our intent being based on universal love.
According to Thoth Raismes (as translated by Maia Nartoomid):

"The Earth and other worlds are created as a path for karmic resolution to prevent certain forces from building within the sacred trinity of Pleiades, Sirius and Orion whereby the pure thresholds of Light might become violated in time. These worlds including the Earth are created within a parallel construct of the *Ranna* Time Flow, but still aligned to it"

There are many different points or nodes of interface between the *Ranna* Time Flow (the Metatronic Universes) and our linear time reality. Places on the earth where the veil between time realities is thin are often called portals. If they are earth nodes that allow access into the Metatronic more real time continuum known as the *Ranna* Time Flow then these are valid nodes with which the Reshel "light technology" may interface.

In the Rosslyn area the ley lines frequently interface with the Reshel earth grids, usually on key points or nodes defined by the geometry of the Reshel. Metatronic ley lines within grids that conform to Reshel forms are an essential ingredient in the "return home" as well as in the realization of the objectives for the creation of this Continuum in the first place. Earth is now rapidly moving away from the Oritronic range of light into the full light again (in its lower range), but in the process has to undergo a lot of clearing of old energies – hence the surge of wars and pollution and societal confusion and breakdown. These disruptive actions are the "dross" that is released by individuals and organizations, released due to the high energy exposure worldwide. In addition to this natural process of clearing there are also evil agencies active in opposition to the Ascension. The secret is to see beyond the dross being released and other various forms of disruption, and find the signs of new emerging consciousness that is aligned with the Metatronic range of frequencies.

These energy frequencies are far, far greater than we are accustomed to. The Metatronic "light codes" are not measurable, as they are outside of linear time. Linear measurements are becoming less applicable, as quantum measurements and other laws come into play. In quantum physics new discoveries indicate the top end of the Oritronic range is being accessed, as indeed the Oritronic frequencies have to transmute and fall away in order to make this paradigm shift. Humanity will carry through the best practices and the Metatronic quality of wisdom learned from our old Oritronic ways into the future, for Earth supplies the arena where this great human experiment plays out – to see if we can learn to recreate the divine order.

The wisdom of this Continuum-experience will merge with our valid Past to create the Future already made (but which is dynamic and growing). Our sense of the divine order has never fully left us. In the future, we will not only sense the divine process of creation, but partake in it consciously. For this to occur we need to understand that we are becoming divine, slowly, over aeons of time.

Once again there are signs of people wishing to make connections between all sentient beings, not content to swallow the piecemeal and non-co-operative existence the mass media and more archaic institutions present. The Metatronic reality that people are experiencing as they awaken to the higher realities includes instant manifestation and many routine phenomena that we now relate to as miraculous. These include levitation, bilocation, teleportation, telepathy, no disease or evil, organ regeneration, death only as a planned event for convenience and a graceful ceremony. This is new to most people but we are becoming aware of more of this as Ascension levels increase.

If ever the old Templar mission of creating Heaven on Earth were to reverberate, Now is the time.

Reshel Earth Grids

The Reshel pattern, along with other grids, are installed for a specific purpose within the overall thrust for Earth's giant shift in consciousness and higher state of being commonly called the Ascension or "Transition". It is also apparent that the Planet as a sentient being "Gaia" also shapes systems to adjust to her evolution; this is a synergic effort combining the realms of devic, angelic and human ensouled beings. The effects of the Reshel grids tend to last longer than the likes of grids exhibiting simple geometric patterns like the chakra grids. This is due to its essential Metatronic resonance with the Earth and Humanity and its capability to adjust at every degree of evolution. Once installed it can contract, expand, flash on and off, duplicate itself elsewhere temporarily, invert, implode and so on. Most of this amazing activity is in the etheric and mental planes but will ground in the physical world at key sites, and thus we humans can interact with the natural and "artefact" grids. The primary points that fix its pattern provide the base that links with the primary intent of the system in place, and thereafter it is free to move according to what its function dictates. Each node in the geometry of the Reshel represents a spiritual function that works synergistically with the other nodes. Humans, along with angelic and elemental agencies can operate the systems, and even install them in their own light bodies as "add-ons."

You can view the grid as a divine thought form. (It is a "Metatronic" system so the level of divinity is at least at the level of Metatron the highest archangel). Its detailed spiritual functions were gleaned from inner journeying by specialist spiritual groups in the past. These groups linked with mentors on the inner planes in order to access knowledge.

Synergy Group Light Process using Reshel formats

The Reshel is in effect a Hebrew term given to a universal form of spiritual system that shares ancient Celtic and Hebrew Judeo-Christian roots, and was applied in some of the mystery schools and temples in ancient Egypt and long before that too, until it last surfaced on a large scale with the inner mystical core of the Knights Templar, and then the early Masons. Nowadays the Reshel is used in geometric formations intrinsic to synergic group exercises in light work, as a safe bridge to the higher dimensions in which the highest spiritual energies available to mankind reside. The synergy groups appear to be an intrinsic part of an overall Ascension program – as it unfolds, ancient grids are upgraded as well as new ones are manifested, all of which come on-line within the Planetary and Racial collective Mind/Soul.

This Reshel method generates certain universal symbols and thought forms, and it is interesting to note that the Templars and Masons were the last large collective human group to utilise the Reshel forms. The Bible contains many references to the science. However we observe that few, if any, clerics are aware of it. Buehler's thought is that the science was largely erased from the Racial Mind in the late 1800s and then restarted in the early 1970s. He believes that the established groups appear to be too strongly entrained in their traditions to be able to adjust to Ascension dynamics which require releasing of major systems designed for a Universe that is rapidly transitioning into a new spiritual-science.

The early builders and operators understood the long-term requirements of Ascension and thus incorporated these essential divine thought forms represented by specific geometric (non–physical) light patterns into the designs of certain cathedral and other temple designs they were associated with within their network, and even aligned sites across vast tracts of land. For the most part the earth grids are ancient but are reenergized when needed, as they have been for this Time.

The Reshel crosses all time, geographical, religious and cultural barriers. That is why Templar symbols can be detected in older cultures across the world. One local artist Nicola Moss contacted me after reading an article I wrote on the Reshel ley lines in a regional magazine. Nicola saw in the symbols and patterns a strong link with her own inner journeying. She writes:

"I contacted Jackie, as I had for some years been drawing images that came to my mind's eye, while sitting quietly in chosen places in the landscape. I had noticed some places were more fertile, producing very luminous images, while other places produced very little or nothing. I asked Jackie about this and she was sure it depended on the local natural energy flows. The images that arise are symbolic. They have no fixed meaning in themselves, but are there to resonate on many levels - personal, cultural or Archetypal. Symbols are like keys that may unlock doors to new areas of knowledge and understanding. They have a timeless quality, yet they seem to herald future manifestation, near or far, in some form and for me are land marks of affirmation along my path."

Using the Reshel in a synergy group is a highly specialized form of light processing. Modern light groups using synergic technique along with Reshel related systems are using highly specialized techniques. They work with inner dimensional organizations under Metatronic leadership. This also includes angelic interaction. From all indications their light work uses the same process as earlier groups such as the Templars and early Masons, and is at an extremely high level commensurate with the ability of group members to safely use the required energies. By creating structured systems resonant with divine harmonics, greater stability to the energy vortex permits more energy, flexibility, and project subtlety to be applied in the group *merkaba* field by the inner-dimensional mentors.

This mode of light work differs from most light groups that are "entrained", meaning they employ chanting, or a suggestion of what you may visualize, or use other methods that will entrain the members into one thought-form matrix (all thinking the same thing) - in a Reshel process the group is made of individuals who each bring their own spiritual gifts to form a unified whole, and then allow the spiritual work to unfold in a "free-flow pattern" with the intention of connecting with the highest possible realms in Earth and cosmos. The "synergic" idea is that the members are holding individual positions in the Unity, thus permitting great flexibility in making very rapid changes in configurations, reorientation, individual pole's energy surge, etc... Entrainment virtually eliminates separate poles. These rapid changes in a group process are controlled by inner planes angelic or Hierarchical "team" members who perceive and adjust energy and thought forms, in order to streamline the process set by current spiritual objectives. Physical people could not manage this process alone due to the speed and precision demanded.

By using a "free-flow" technique intense connections are made, and images are received according to the level and quality of grace, clarity of the group and their intent in unity with inner planes "team mates". There are other variables such as the member's ability to process high frequencies and intensity. The light training begins with a form known as the Key (or Shield) of David, which is essentially a six pointed star that incorporates the key nodes in the basic geometry. The group vortex is initially organized by using the simple geometric form; this in turn increases stability, as well as triggering the etheric formation of a Star Tetrahedron or "tetratryon" used in the creation and communication sequencing. Other systems may also be inserted by the inner planes team.

Light work using Reshel formats is only conducted after the essential silence has been reached in which greater accuracy and relevance can emerge. This silence is called the "Selah" in Hebrew. The Selah is translated as "….the silence between musical notes and the unmoving fulcrum in scales"... used in the inner-planes to relate to the Silence, Rest, of the Unmanifest God. This state of being provides the Life in phenomena and is foundational to all actions.

Psalm 75:3
"The earth and all the inhabitants thereof are dissolved: I bear up the pillars of it. Selah."

As over the aeons the objectives are to assist the angels and elemental beings in ensuring the creative evolution of our planet, which requires creating the prime conditions for the return of Earth on all sentient levels to a more evolved state or vibration known as the Metatronic realm, where the highest archangel Metatron dwells. Within the Metatronic realm, time and space do not exist, and the formations used in Reshel light work that reach into this state of no time/ space deploy a safe protective mode. The archangel Michael presides over our current epoch. To emphasize, the Reshel is not primarily an outward event, although it creates Form, - in Essence it is describing an inner state of **active silence** (a Moving-Selah) in which the mysteries of creation are revealed, employed and extended. The astounding complexity and speed of Creation

Dynamics demands that "Absolute Simplicity" (the Moving-Selah) be used to make all needed connections in dimensions, agencies, events across and out of Time, et al.

Other Applications of the Reshel

The Reshel apparently provides an interface between the linear world we live in normally and the divine world of light. Such external manifestations of the inner synergic work are an adjunct to understanding how the system works. The synergic group practice deploys the most complex Reshel forms as applied by the group's mentors on the inner planes. The practice yields a vast array of universal symbols and energy patterns over time. Buehler then applies the insights gained from the synergic meditation practices to his geometric study of earth grids, temples, cathedrals and other human artefacts in the world.

As a body of metaphysical knowledge the Reshel as an etheric overlaying template can be found in a variety of applications in recent centuries. Through his inner efforts and his conducting and interpreting of synergy group processes over decades, Buehler progressively realised the composite spiritual functions of various Reshel patterns, and was able to analyse a growing range of artefacts such as ancient temples, medieval cathedrals, early heraldry and stone carvings, early Masonic paintings, crop circles, independent researchers' work in sacred geometry, architecture etc. Those who created the artefacts may not have realised that their work was encoded with the Reshel at the time of creation, but if they were constructing under divine inspiration the net result is that the Reshel coding is present.

Esoteric knowledge was evidently known to those who designed Rosslyn, and Buehler believes they practised the specialist form of synergic meditation there and arranged for the construction of monuments across Europe that mapped out the matrix of leys and grids. The inner core of Templars at Rosslyn intended the chapel to act as a beacon in the future, facilitating changes in the way people think and connect with the truth. Due to the astronomical movements taking place now there is little doubt the Templars as keen observers of the skies and related Time-lines anticipated that our present times would herald many changes that would be crucial for the fulfilment for the purpose of Rosslyn (see Appendix F).

Reshel Patterns in and around Rosslyn Chapel

Rosslyn Chapel is a miniscule but perfect example of Reshel patterning, enabling highly efficient contact with the higher spiritual realms. The geometric forms it deploys are the closest yet most compacted representation of divine energies/light forms/thought patterns available to humanity according to William Buehler. The chapel is a microcosm of Reshel codes while the local landscape is a macrocosm encoded with the Reshel that expands into a system of leys spanning the continents. Sites nearby exhibiting and using the Reshel system include Stonehenge, Chartres, Montserrat and the more modern structure Chiswick House in London! At such sites they act as temples of light, with various key buildings or sites in the immediate area surrounding them that anchor and expand the sites with a matrix or pattern of ley lines. The main sites interconnect through the various Reshel grids, and act like major modules in a vast spiritual machine intended to drive the evolutionary jump.

The Rosslyn area was and is shared by many of these European grids, and is more significant than many of the Reshel areas world-wide for many reasons. The ancient Reshel matrix is expanding at a very fast, if not exponential rate and Rosslyn is at the epicentre of much of the Reshel activity world-wide. Ongoing research in light work and into local landscape alignments suggest that the ancient sacred patterns of the Reshel are producing new patterns, indicating that the Earth and collective race as a synergic sentient being is preparing for a great transition that can positively affect mankind.

In Buehler's words:

"The Roslin immediate area is a very intense and ancient site focusing Metatronic dynamics."

Roslin Glen adjacent to the chapel with its River North Esk running through the steep sandstone gorge is a very energetic elemental area. The chapel and glen have to be taken as one composite whole. (We are told by Thoth that there have been three major temples in the site, before the present Chapel and Glen, since the last of Atlantis went down.) Major systems were put in place during the era of Atlantis anticipating a progressive evolution leading to the present Transition. The Atlans knew of this Land as "Alba-On" the "Bridging Place." Thoth notes that the fuller meaning was "to succor, gather, feed, unite or bridge." We believe that this Land was the ancient bridge from the lost Atlan civilization to this last 12,000 years of our present culture, now again in a bridging process.

Rosslyn as a Green Chapel and a Serpent Temple

Rosslyn is the ultimate Green Chapel, since one of its main spiritual purposes is to (re)unite the elemental or devic realms with the human realm as a vital part of creating the New Race that is made up of the qualities of all three realms in the real Universes.

One of the main spiritual themes Rosslyn develops is that of regeneration that the Green Men carvings in the chapel remind us of. Similarly the serpent is represented by the Hebrew letter Nun which means "Regenerating life" and will be examined later. The pillar widely known as the Apprentice Pillar is connected to this theme by a geometric radial discussed later too. From the base of the pillar the eight serpents send forth the greenery that entwines the masonry of the chapel. The greenery can be regarded as the quality of eternal regeneration in nature.

The serpent was also known as the worm or "Shamir" whose wisdom was able to split the solid matter and shape the stone used to build the Temple of Solomon in Arab and Rabbinic legend (see Andrew Sinclair's book The Sword and the Grail for an excellent description of this). Since on a surface level Rosslyn is seen to be replicating the original Temple, the serpent motif would indeed be a strong design feature of the chapel. On a deeper level, having encoded the chapel with the Reshel, the chapel in its etheric form lies outside of linear time in the greater reality of a "no time" frame in the Metatronic world, and will respond to each progressive wave of regeneration that occurs.

The Red and the White Paths

There are two realities or paths that humanity straddles and has to deal with at this time; the Red and the White. Inspired by Maia Nartoomid's excellent description of these Paths, Buehler describes them as that of "the Fall and its associative path of Redemption (with its own higher wisdom), and the other of Grace, that is borne of perfection, as the reality resonant with the rest of the universes. Both paths are Grail paths; to Buehler it seems that the Red Path relate to the 'Guardians of the Sacred Heart', or the Warrior-Priest ethic. The Knights-Templar were this by definition. Sacrifice was part of this Path and still is. John 15:12-13 teaches **"This is my commandment: That ye love one another as I have loved you. Greater love hath no man than this: that a man lay down his life for his friends."**

This Red Path dynamic is found in a major ley line system between Holy Island Lindisfarne and the twin islands of Iona and Staffa. According to Thoth this ley line was known as the "Spear of Longinus" as it released the sacred Blood and Water into the Land at Holy-Rood Sanctuary in Edinburgh. An added level of redemption (and sacrifice) is realized if we correlate the islands of Iona and Staffa with the Christos and Lucifer "Star-Gates", effectively the major poles generating this Continuum reality. The strong White Path complement is found in the vital Grail

Presence at Glastonbury Tor; this is a pole that connects with Edinburgh in forming an amazing Grail system between them. The polar couplet is an excellent example of the two Paths working in concert. Thoth noted that the "Spear of Longinus" system and function was known to St Columba and his monks, who used it in combination with the thought form of the Crucifixion over Edinburgh and flow of redemptive transformation through the Edinburgh grid system in which Rosslyn is the Resh pole (Chief Head Stone). We note that the Roman soldier, Longinus, (according to Thoth) was a competent master of spiritual alchemy and a part of the larger Event. Longinus is another example of the Warrior-Priest ethic.

The earth is linked to the White Path by our past and future continua in the *Ranna* Wave of higher reality. We are being required to rapidly shift our balance, in this "straddling" posture, and move solidly onto the path of Grace in the Christic/ Metatronic reality. Buehler says

"Rosslyn and many other temples were designed to handle the new, and real, continua with the basic installation of the Reshel format. This is the one harmonic system most adapted to facilitating the actual continuum shift. So I see Rosslyn, and the other temples, not only as coming into their old and superior application but now into their real and intended potential. She's coming into her new life..... Since 2005 Rosslyn has made an essential shift from a main function of redemption to one of full realization or 'resurrection'. In this it will be coming into its originally intended potential"."

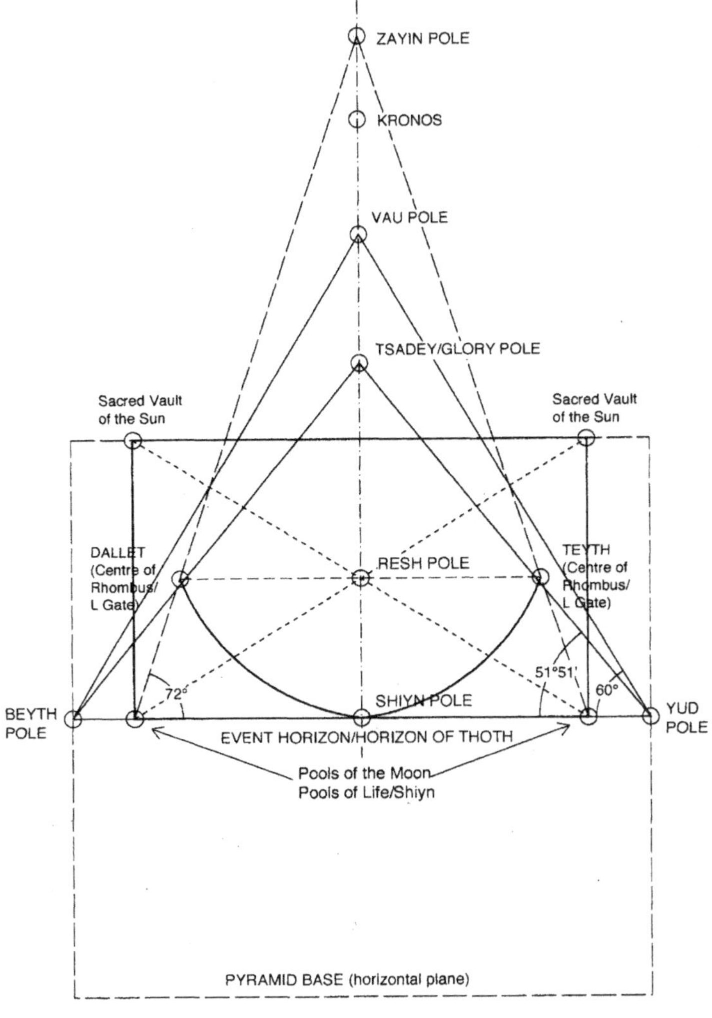

FIGURE 1 : THE FEMALE HALF OF THE RESHEL
SHOWING BASIC POLES
ZAYIN POLE
KRONOS
VAU POLE
TSADEY/GLORY POLE
Sacred Vault
of the Sun
Sacred Vault
of the Sun
DALLET
(Centre of
Rhombus/
L Gate)
RESH POLE
TEYTH
(Centre of
Rhombus/
L Gate)
51°51'
72°
60°
SHIYN POLE
BEYTH
POLE
YUD
POLE
EVENT HORIZON/HORIZON OF THOTH
Pools of the Moon
Pools of Life/Shiyn
PYRAMID BASE (horizontal plane)

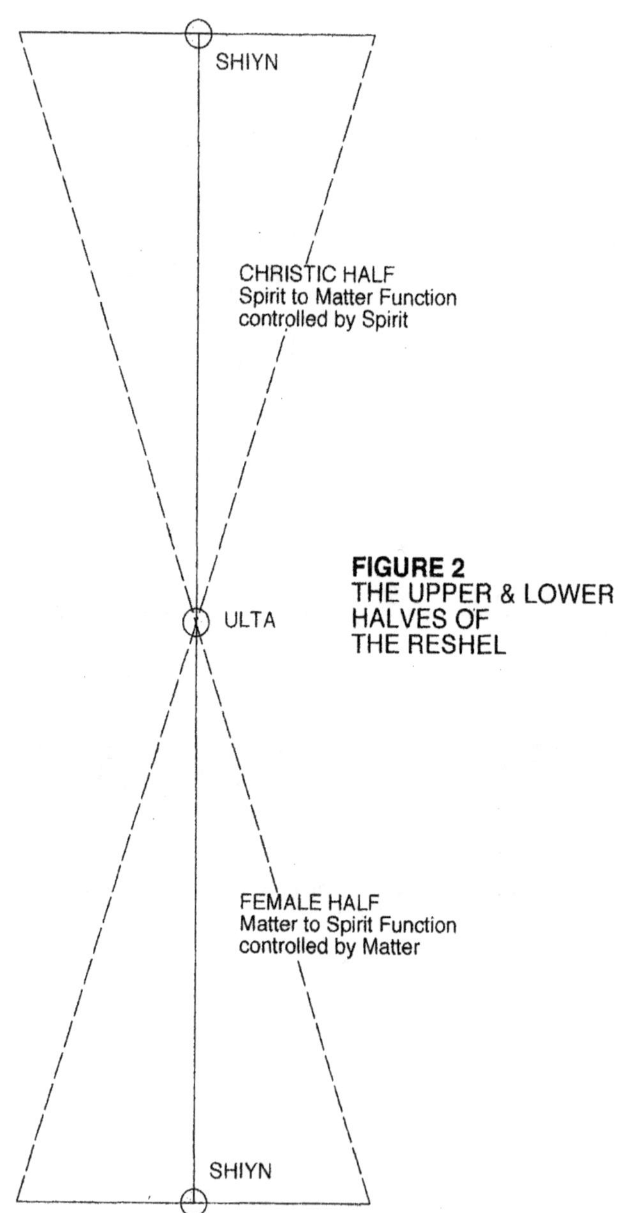

FIGURE 2
THE UPPER & LOWER
HALVES OF
THE RESHEL

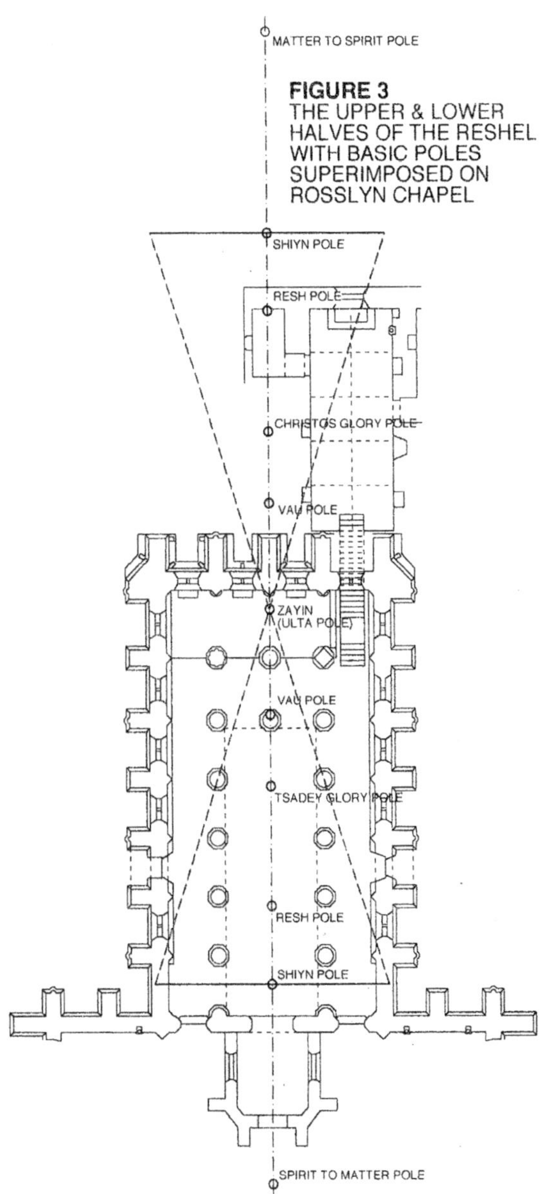

FIGURE 3
THE UPPER & LOWER
HALVES OF THE RESHEL
WITH BASIC POLES
SUPERIMPOSED ON
ROSSLYN CHAPEL

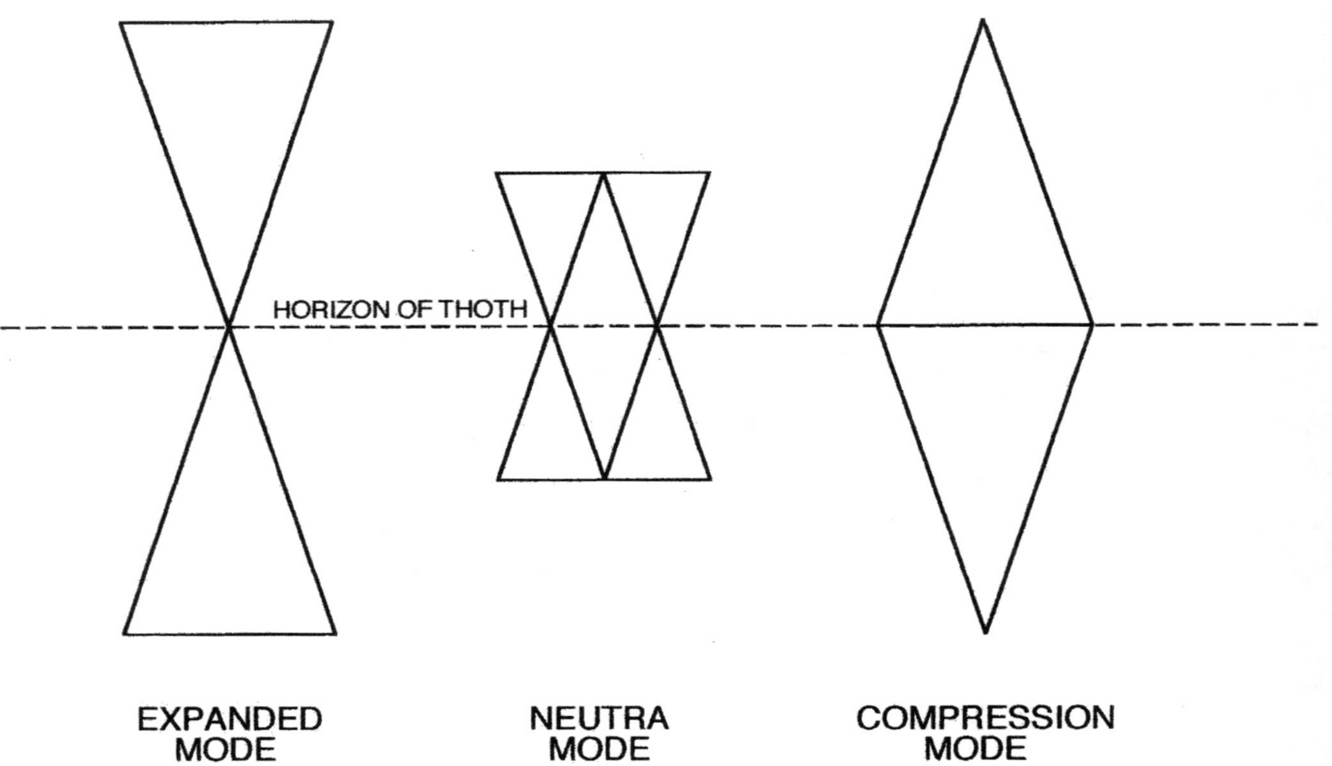

FIGURE 4 : THE PRINCIPAL MODES OF REALITY

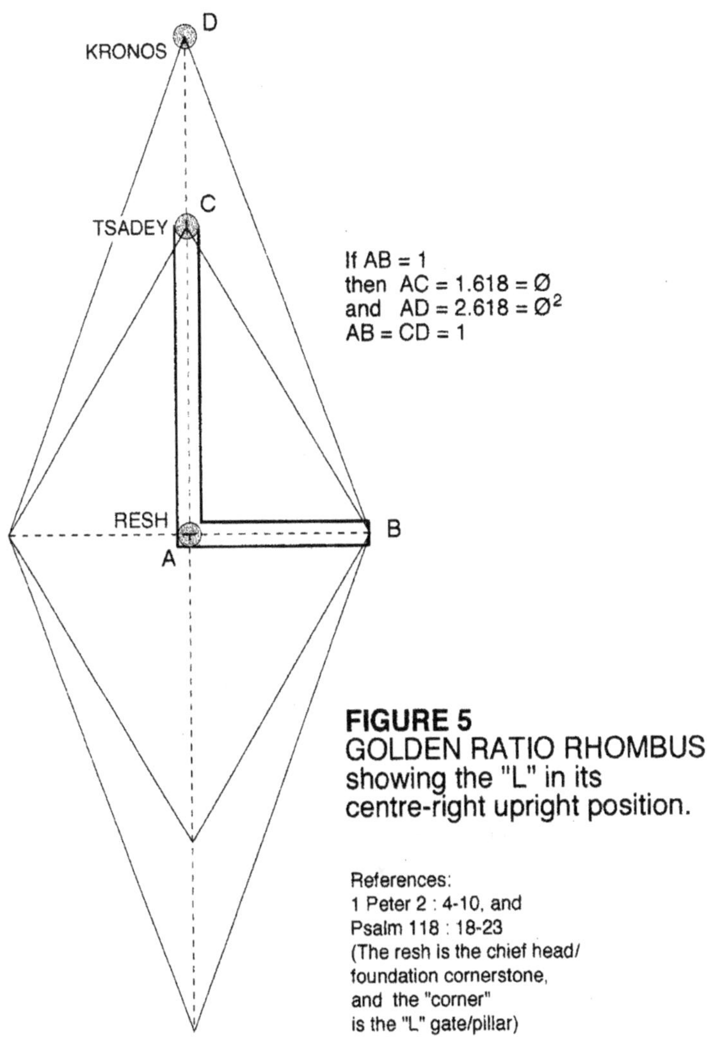

FIGURE 5
GOLDEN RATIO RHOMBUS
showing the "L" in its
centre-right upright position.

References:
1 Peter 2 : 4-10, and
Psalm 118 : 18-23
(The resh is the chief head/
foundation cornerstone,
and the "corner"
is the "L" gate/pillar)

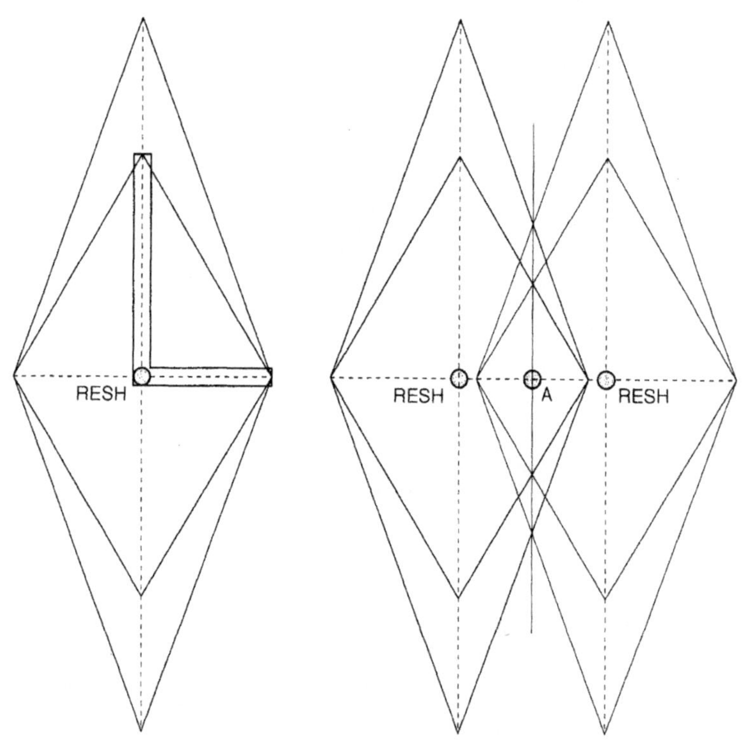

FIGURE 6 : TWO GOLDEN RATIO RHOMBUSES, SHOWING THE
NEW RESH POINT WHERE THEY INTERSECT AT "A"

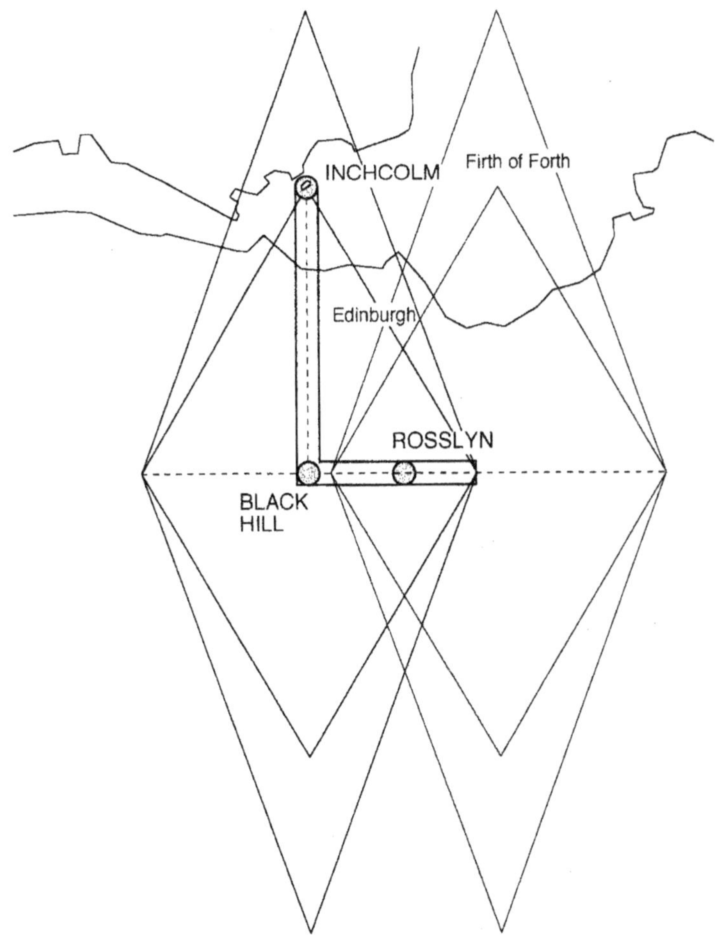

FIGURE 7 : TWO GOLDEN RATIO RHOMBUSES
AND THE "L", WITH ROSSLYN AT THE
RESH POINT WHERE THEY INTERSECT

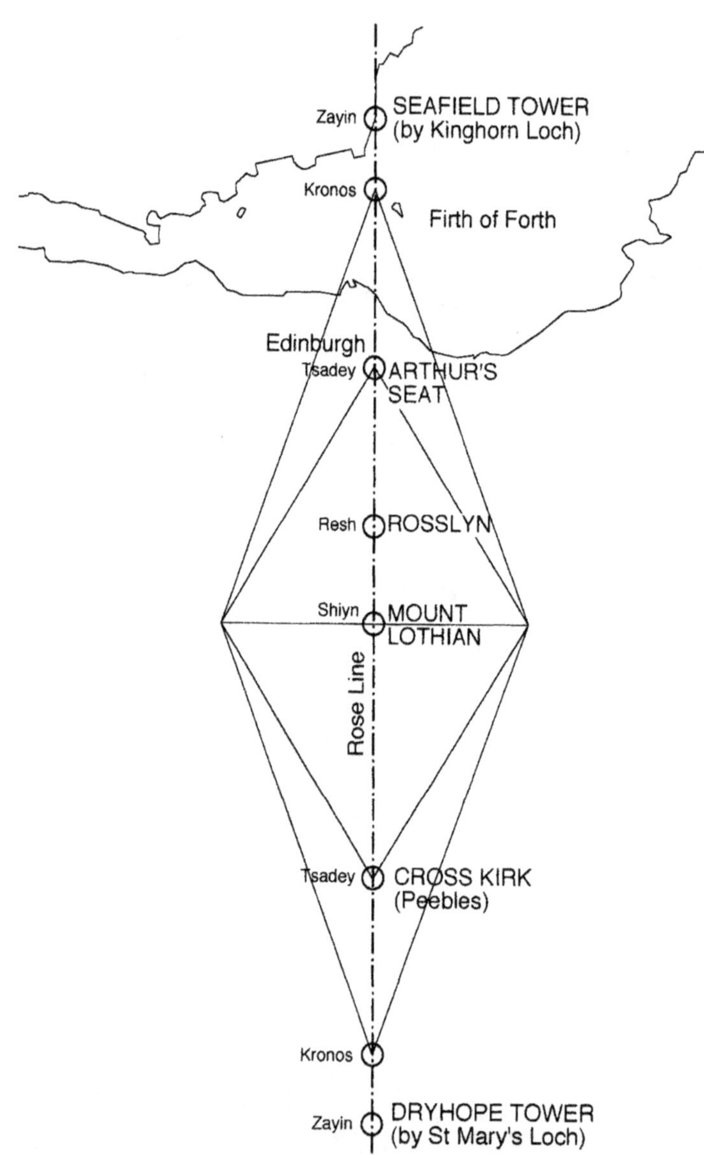

FIGURE 8 : ROSE LINE PASSING THROUGH
EDINBURGH GRID, SHOWING
POLES OF BASIC RESHEL

28

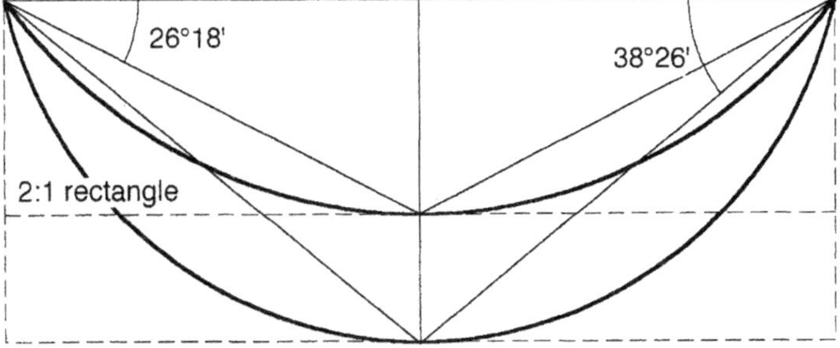

ANGLES INVOLVED IN SINCLAIR CROSS

The flatter curve is constructed using an angle of 26°18', while the outer curve matches that shown in the original Sinclair Cross in the Chapel, below, which yields an angle of 38°26'.

It is quite impractical to construct the 'corners' at the crossing of the Sinclair Cross, as shown below, using the flatter curve.

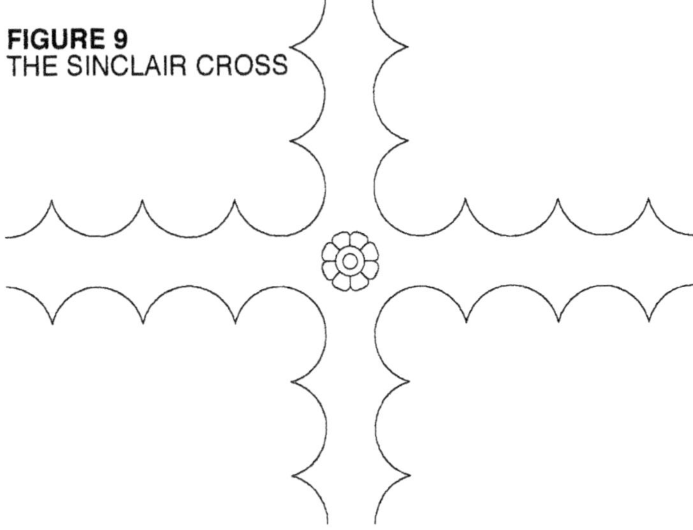

FIGURE 9
THE SINCLAIR CROSS

FIGURE 10
THE RESH WITHIN THE CHRISTIC HALF OF THE
GOLDEN RHOMBUS (set in Rosslyn Lower Chapel)

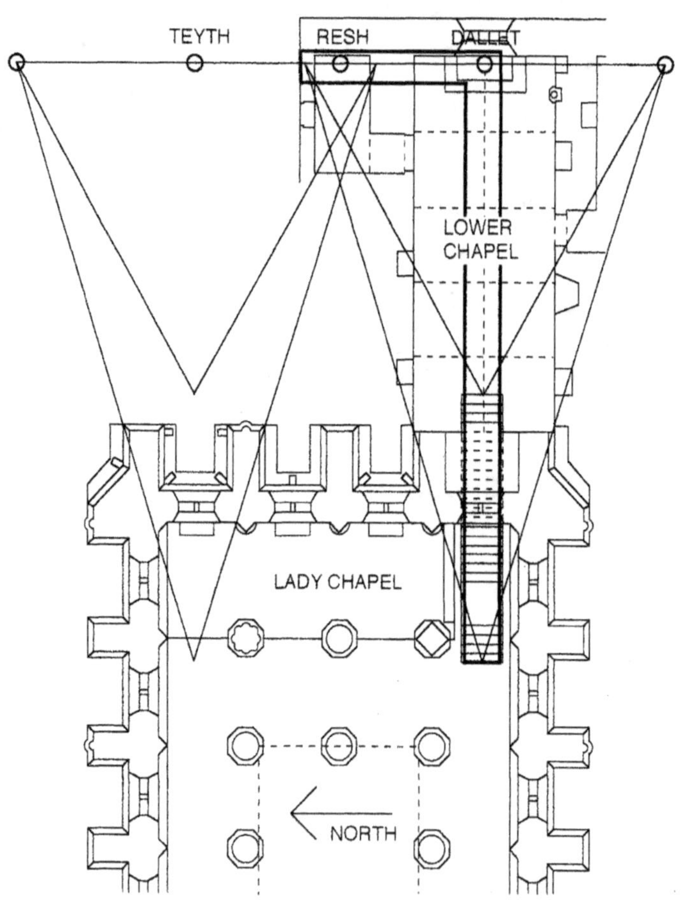

TEYTH
RESH
DALLET
LOWER
CHAPEL
LADY CHAPEL
NORTH

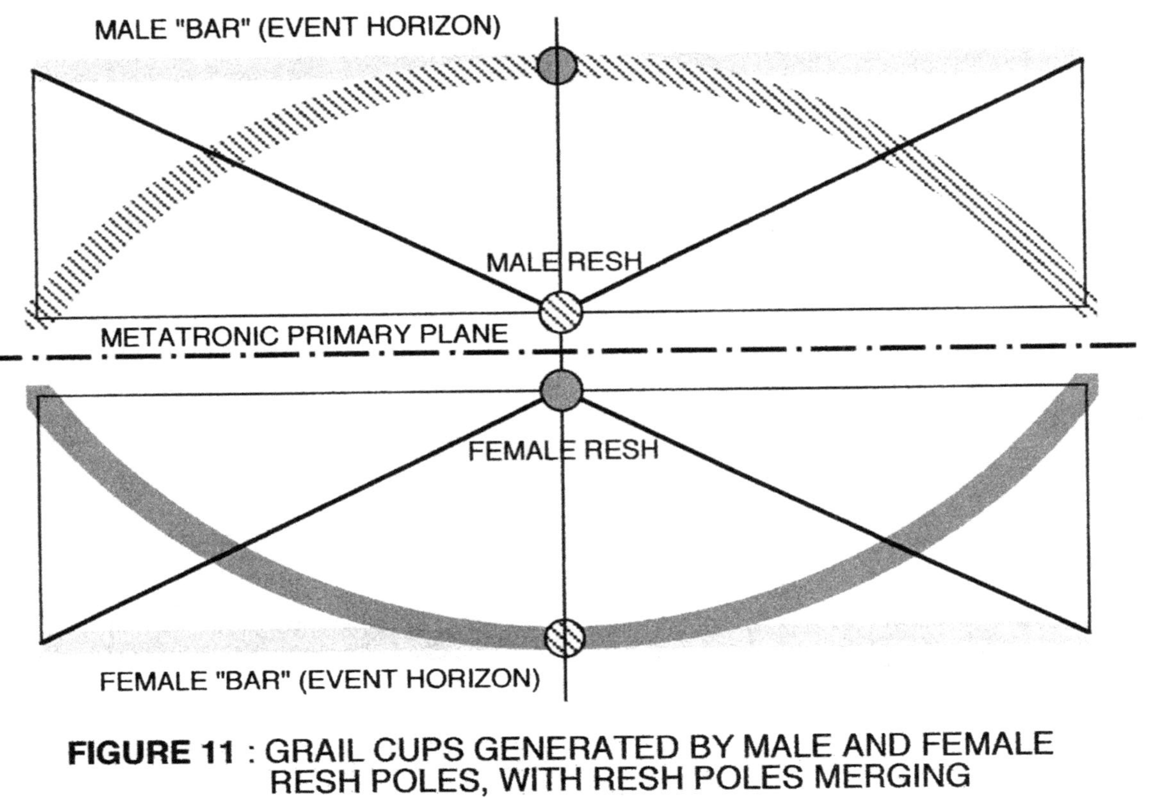

FIGURE 11 : GRAIL CUPS GENERATED BY MALE AND FEMALE RESH POLES, WITH RESH POLES MERGING

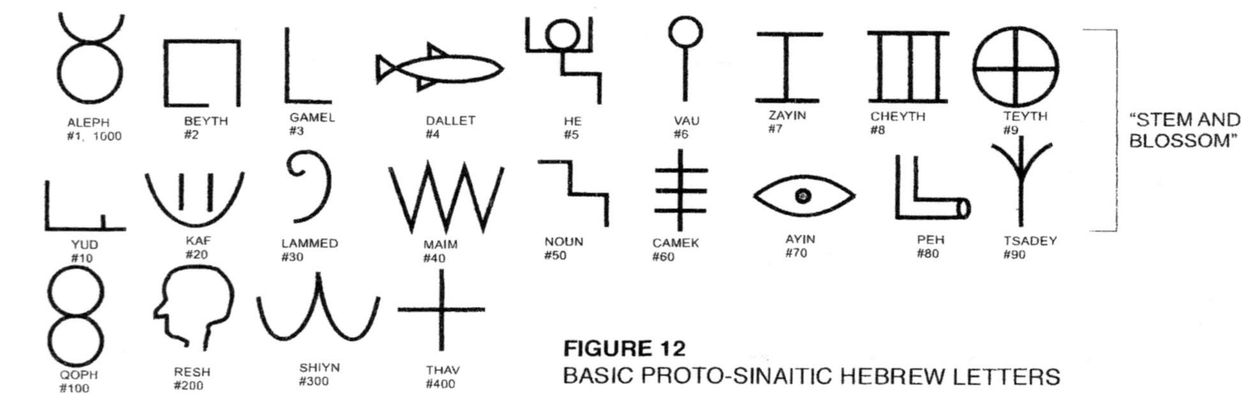

FIGURE 12
BASIC PROTO-SINAITIC HEBREW LETTERS

NOTE: These glyphs are not all consistently presented in historical references, so I have slightly adjusted some. I have also assumed some meanings not found in current translations. My assumptions are from my own experience in their applications. Do not use this graphic in an 'academic' project without doing your own research.

William Buehler

FIGURE 13 : THE MAIN EAST WINDOW AT ROSSLYN CHAPEL

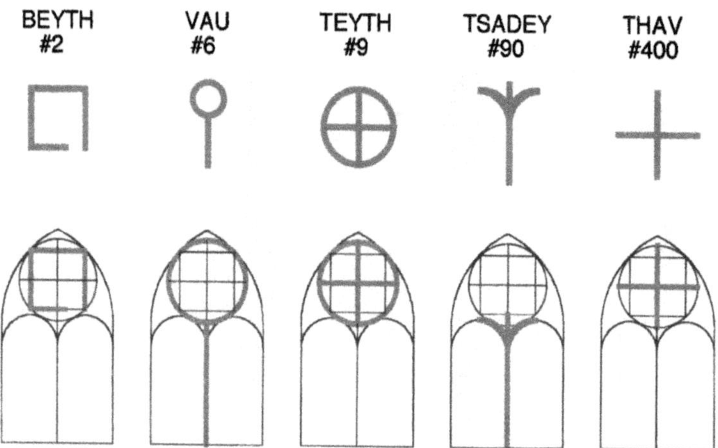

FIGURE 14 : ANALYSIS OF PROTO-SINAITIC HEBREW LETTERS
CONTAINED IN THE TRACERY OF THE WINDOW

FIGURE 15 : SYNTHESIS
DEVELOPMENT OF THE PATTERN IN THE WINDOW

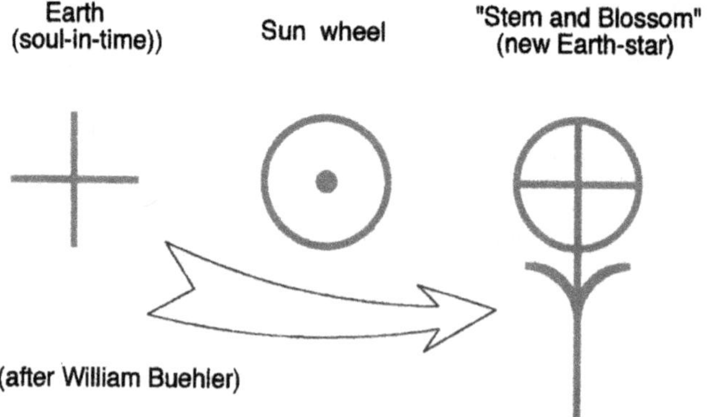

34

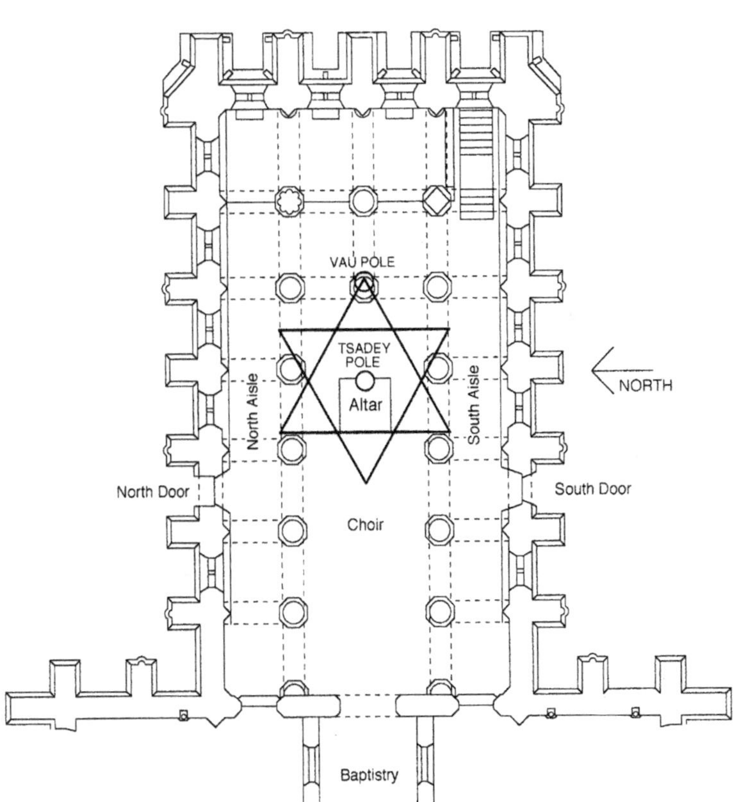

FIGURE 16 : STAR OF DAVID CENTRED
ON THE ALTAR AT ROSSLYN

FIGURE 17 : EASTERN PART OF ROSSLYN CHAPEL
SHOWING 8 DIRECTIONS OF THE TEMPLA MAR

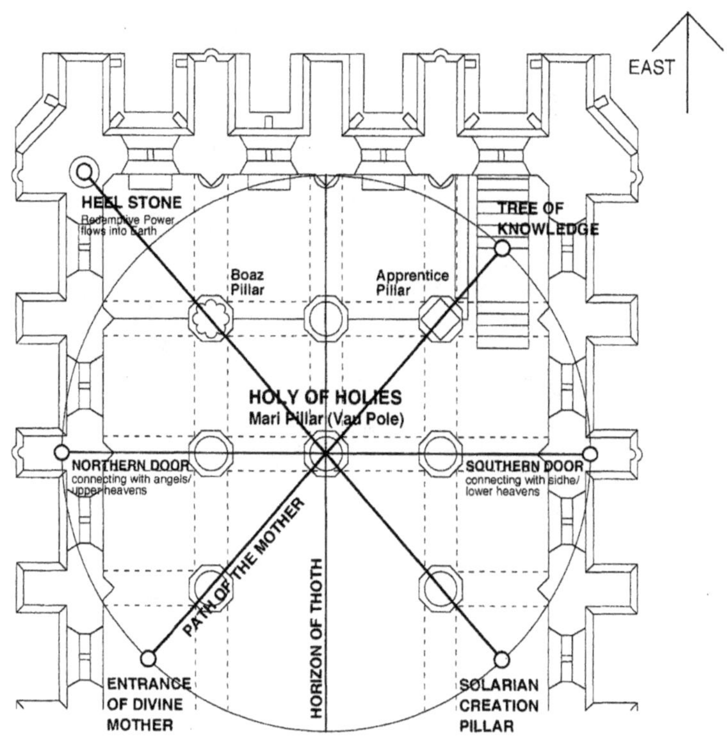

EAST
HEEL STONE
Redemptive Power flows into Earth
TREE OF KNOWLEDGE
Boaz Pillar
Apprentice Pillar
HOLY OF HOLIES
Mari Pillar (Vau Pole)
NORTHERN DOOR
connecting with angels/ upper heavens
SOUTHERN DOOR
connecting with sidhe/ lower heavens
PATH OF THE MOTHER
HORIZON OF THOTH
ENTRANCE OF DIVINE MOTHER
SOLARIAN CREATION PILLAR

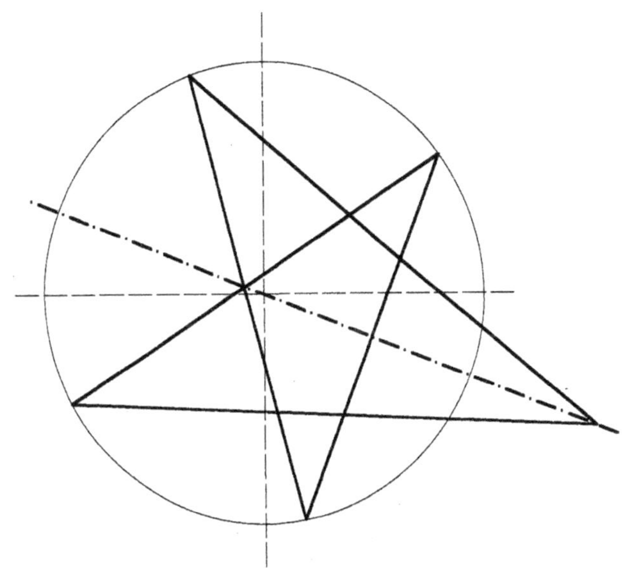

FIGURE 18 : PENTAGRAM WITH AN ELONGATED ARM

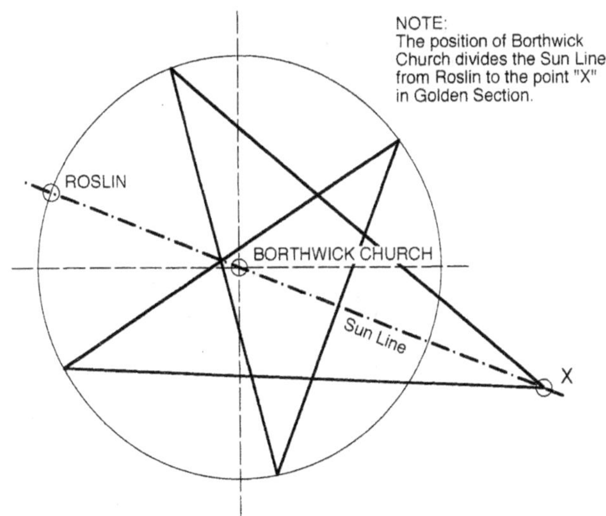

FIGURE 19 : PENTAGRAM SHOWING THE SUN LINE
FROM ROSLIN THROUGH BORTHWICK
CHURCH WHERE HELIOTROPE IS CENTRED

FIGURE 20
BASIC RESHEL SYSTEM CENTRED ON
EAST WALL OF ROSSLYN, ON ROSE LINE

CHRISTIC HALF
TELEPLANE/
EVENT HORIZON
ULTA
POLE
ROSE LINE
(tav hara)
FEMALE HALF

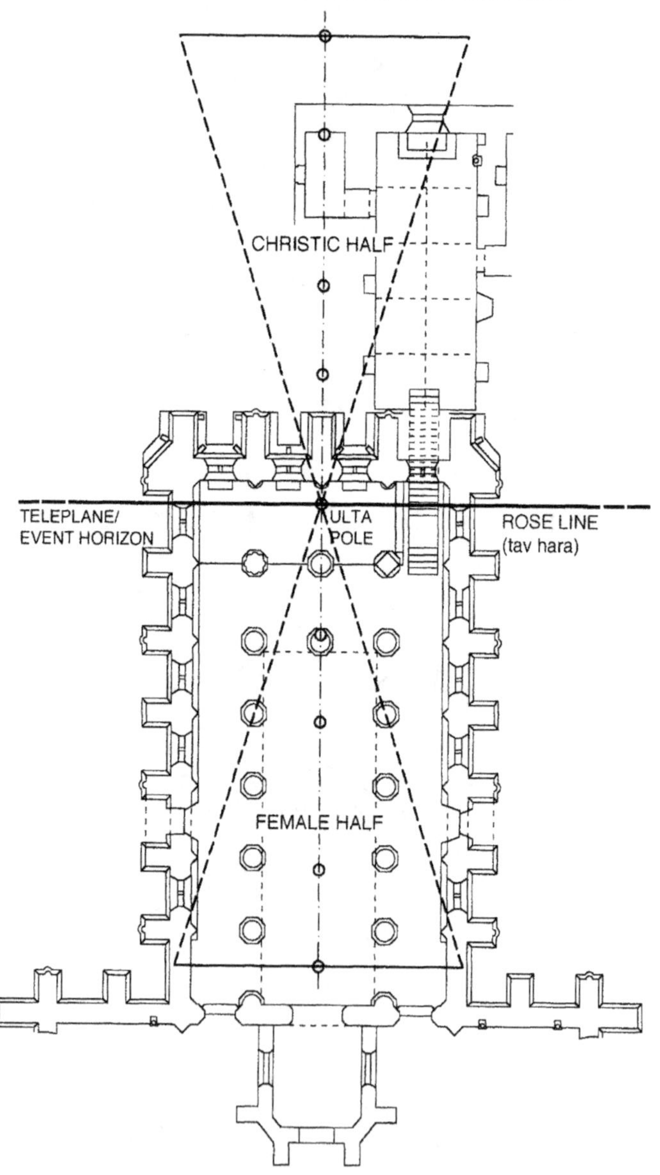

38

FIGURE 21
HIGHER RESHEL SYSTEM CENTRED ON MARI PILLAR & USING APOSTOLIC PLANE

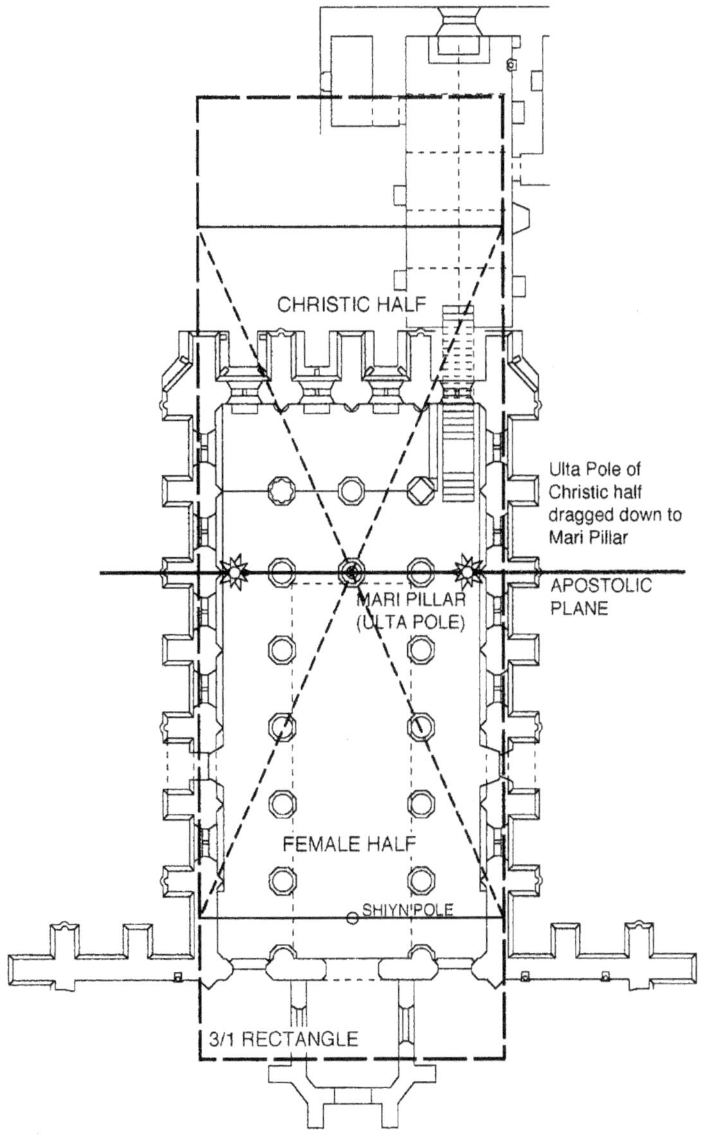

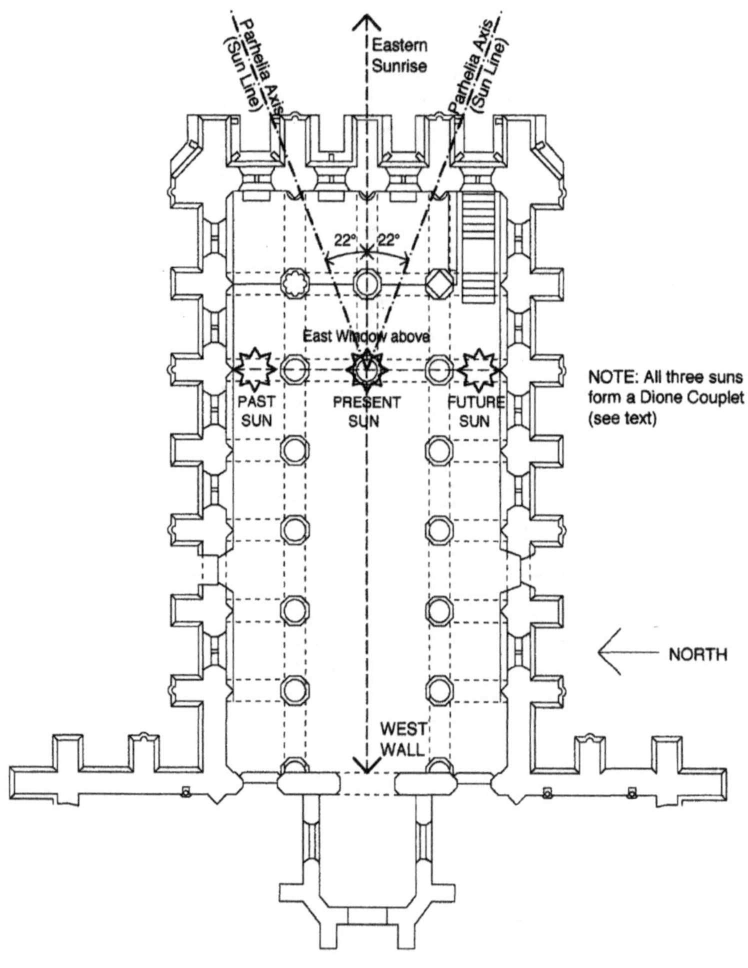

FIGURE 22 : THE PARHELIA AXES
IN RELATION TO ROSSLYN CHAPEL
Parhelia Axis (Sun Line)
Parhelia Axis (Sun Line)
Eastern Sunrise
22°
22°
East Window above
PAST SUN
PRESENT SUN
FUTURE SUN
NOTE: All three suns form a Dione Couplet (see text)
NORTH
WEST WALL

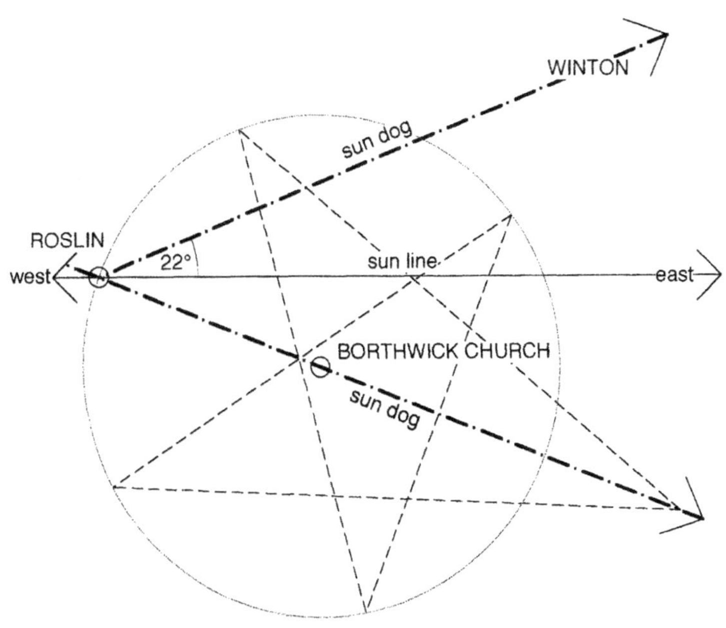

FIGURE 23 : TWO LEYLINES FROM ROSLIN ALONG
PARHELIA AXES IN THE LANDSCAPE

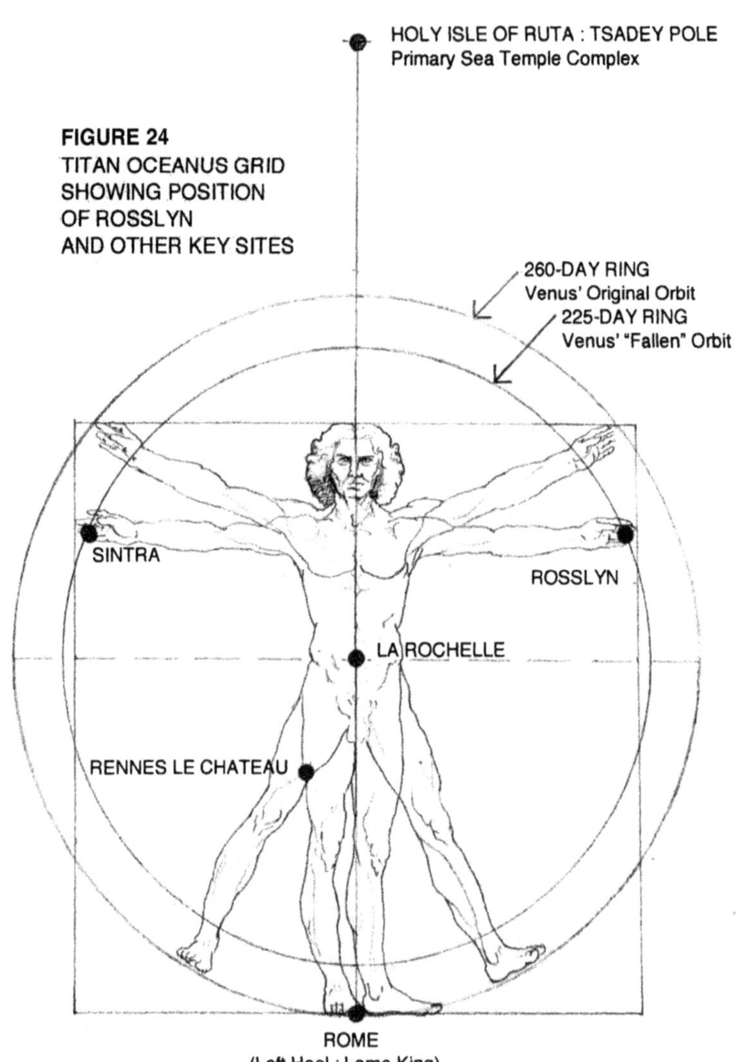

HOLY ISLE OF RUTA : TSADEY POLE
Primary Sea Temple Complex
FIGURE 24
TITAN OCEANUS GRID
SHOWING POSITION
OF ROSSLYN
AND OTHER KEY SITES
260-DAY RING
Venus' Original Orbit
225-DAY RING
Venus' "Fallen" Orbit
SINTRA
ROSSLYN
LA ROCHELLE
RENNES LE CHATEAU
ROME
(Left Heel : Lame King)

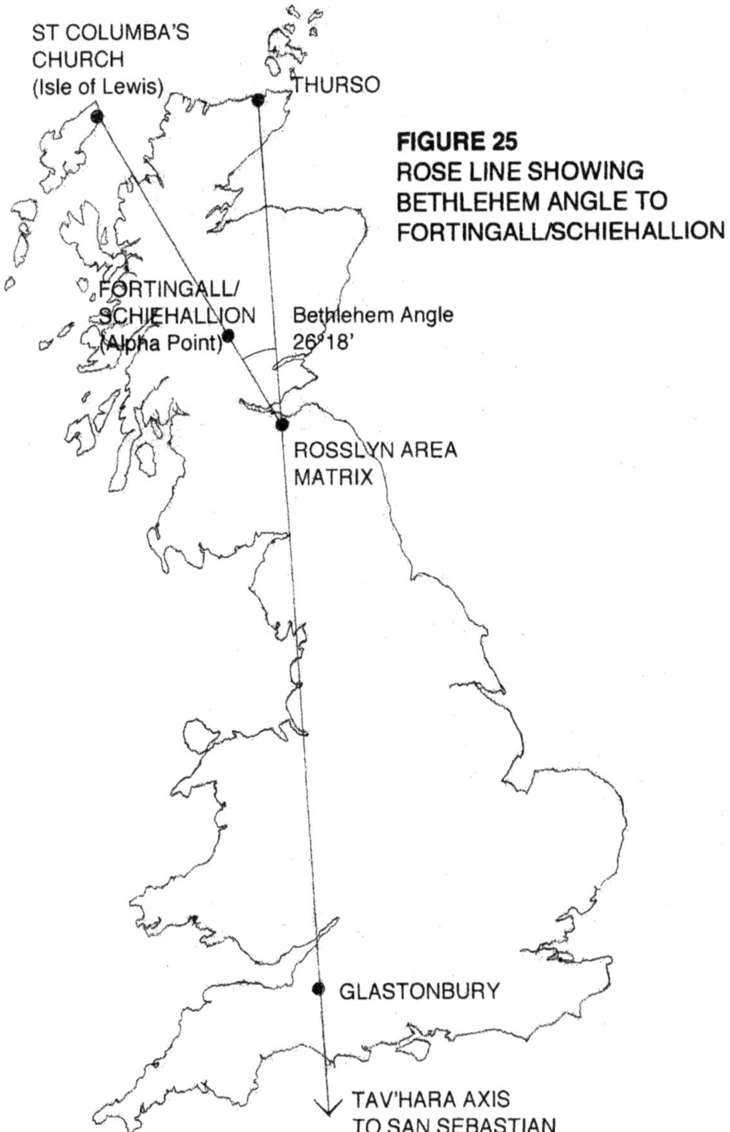

FIGURE 25
ROSE LINE SHOWING
BETHLEHEM ANGLE TO
FORTINGALL/SCHIEHALLION

Chapter Two: Rosslyn and the Reshel

The Reshel as a Basic Template

As an example of such a coded building, Rosslyn Chapel provides the most perfect and yet compact example of the Reshel geometry even though it was never completed. Rosslyn is also of great importance for the continent of Europe and beyond in terms of its geographical and geometric positioning. At least some members of the Sinclairs whose clan chief resided at Rosslyn Castle in successive generations from 1070 until 1778 appeared to have known of these nodes and sited their various strongholds according to this knowledge, as well as applying the same esoteric principles of geometry to their temple at Rosslyn. The Sinclairs are well documented for their wealth, wide trading and cultural connections throughout Europe and even North American maritime explorations. Their access to a wide geographical area allowed them to seed Reshel geometric patterns on land and sea which are in effect pure thought forms that link in with the highest divine light, and can be called light codes for short. Henry Sinclair, the grandfather of the founder of the chapel when he sailed to Nova Scotia in 1398 would have taken the Reshel codes there for regeneration on that continent – this spiritual viewpoint is not necessarily shared by the current Sinclairs.

The basic geometry of the Reshel will be illustrated next. In the same way as the poles are present in buildings such as Rosslyn, there are male and female poles within the landscape that are determined by geometric nodes. Not all the nodes marked in the following diagram will be elaborated on in this book, but for all intents and purposes the basic range of nodes is best shown here. See **Figure 1**.

The Reshel schematic is quite complex so it often appears or is drawn as a simple triangle based on the angles of an equal armed pentagon, assuming the viewer knows the symbolic application. This is the key pattern or basic Reshel Third Breastplate in any Reshel format, whether within the land or a building used for spiritual purposes. Its pattern is intrinsically linked to angles contained in both the physical and etheric levels of the Great Pyramid, Grail, tetrahedron, golden ratio rhombus, pentagonal star, and others.

The pattern is alternatively called the Breastplate of Adam Kadmon. It is a fire pictograph, having the potential to spiritually enflame the person who chooses to work with it and carry it. Within the Reshel, the pattern is the third of twenty four breastplates assigned to the high archangel Metatron, and is being used in our time continuum, in line with the current potential of our planet, which is to make a quantum leap into an entirely new paradigm. In modern jargon, the Reshel triangle as a blueprint represents the Metatronic upgrade for our planet.

The Reshel grid supports our efforts and it can safely adjust to individuals or groups in this fallen continuum in their own levels of awareness and evolution. According to Thoth it opens the path into a higher master blueprint of life held in divine teachings called the Torah Or, which appeared to Daniel in the Old Testament. It is interesting that Buehler augments Thoth's explanation by saying that the name Torah Or equates with "the descending dove, translating Light into form and law (the Decalogue/Pentateuch or Torah). The other, Matter to Spirit, (ascending) dove would be the Yonah version, a parallel with wine and fermentation. The Dove can be represented by the pentagram in what is called the "Penta-Dove" or "Star-Dove." The pentagram represents the Universal Seed used by Metatronic agencies to access our fallen reality. All "5-systems" are included in the Penta-Dove mantle and are collectively called the "Dovine Merkaba."
Buehler translates the "Torah Or" as the tor/towr(ah) in Hebrew to be a "dove, guide, a string (line), order or border, a manner (estate), precept (statute, as in the "Torah")." The "Or"

would relate to "light, lightning, fire". This word for dove also means "bull." The bull correspondent would relate to the crescent horns or grail cup and moon crescent in the Reshel system. An outer arch to a window at Rosslyn Chapel has a carving of a descending dove outside which is very close to an Aleph/bull's horns symbol inside, all of which suggests the carvings are translating divine light into forms within a divine harmonic.

The carvings at Rosslyn often appear to be based on these early Hebrew letters with their correlative numbers and combined energetic meanings. Thoth maintains that Hebrew is one of the five universal divine light codes given to Earth. Thoth also concurs that the glyphs contain the Reshel codes. Apparently the Templars also understood this. The carvings in the chapel correlate well with the Reshel. Light codes based on the proto-Sinaitic letters are engrained in the layout and specifics of the carvings, and this book only touches on the subject, which is vast.

Rosslyn as a Reshel Template

The following diagrams show the two basic halves of the Reshel triangle and how they overlay onto Rosslyn Chapel's ground plan. It is important to realize that while this shape is etherically enlarged and anchored in the landscape using Rosslyn and other points in the land as key nodes, the shape constantly changes from moment to moment. It can shift, spin, implode, enlarge, shrink or even duplicate itself for a specific spiritual task… always using the basic formation and sequencing of the grid. In **Figure 2** you see the two halves of the basic Reshel meeting at a shared *Ulta Point*. (When these two halves draw nearer each other the poles will shift and the two halves will eventually overlay and form a Star of David or six-pointed star. In **Figure 2** there are two halves to the Reshel triangle pattern contained within an upward and a downward pointing triangle. The downward pointing triangle is in the Spirit to Matter mode and is also known as the Christic or generally the male half, while the upward pointing triangle is in the Matter to Spirit mode and generally, as the female component, is known as the *Shekinah* or Bride of Christ half. For brevity, only the latter is displayed in **Figure 1**. In **Figure 2** the Zayin poles of the two halves in effect have merged in the *Ulta pole*. When the Reshel is overlain onto the chapel, with the *Ulta poles* of both halves shared, this is how it looks: see **Figure 3**.

Three Principal Modes of Reality

As mentioned earlier, this is also known as the Third Breastplate of Metatron, which includes the Key of David as one of its main subsystems. This shield is an excellent template showing the basic tenets of the creation process (otherwise called the Grail). It is the main interface between the Unmanifest and the Manifest Form, as used in the Reshel.

There is one Aleph or Ulta point/pole in the unmoving centre of the Reshel. The centre is set within a **teleplane** that never moves. This centre is also known as the Horizon of Thoth, or *Event Horizon*. (Future books intended in this series will elaborate on this space and detail how an Ark dynamic has been inserted here as part of a developing complex light process.) The Shiyn poles either side of the teleplane can move in and out, dragging the Reshel form with it to form new shapes. These shapes are akin to vaults that contain specific realities or universes. The two basic Shiyn poles function through the male Christos and the female *Shekinah* codes that the two halves represent. The Shiyn poles transfer a divine state into temporal terms but not linear time. When the two halves are pulled apart so that the Zayin poles are touching, the apices are point to point in the <u>Expanded Mode.</u> When the two halves of the Reshel are base to base and their apices are apart the Reshel is in <u>Compression Mode</u>. When the two halves are completely interpenetrating the Vau poles in both halves of the Reshel come together at the *Ulta pole.*so as to create the <u>Neutra Mode</u>

representing a Neutra Universe. This can be regarded as the highest mode of reality, since nothing is set and all potential exists. See **Figure 4**.

Of course the Reshel is shifting between all three modes of expression of reality constantly, so this separation into just three operative modes is a simplification for purposes of explaining it. The universe is constantly "flashing" from a mode of compression (cube-sphere) to one of expansion (torus) through a neutra mode of neither, which is the Real or Greater Reality. The *Ulta pole* is in the neutra point holding the reference for the universe. All reality frames or teleplanes model the Ulta's dynamics within one universal harmonic. Apparently the Neutra mode is continually refreshed in the Shiyn poles, and the action is continually recycling in the etheric. There are different etheric vaults formed by the different patterns or nodes. At Rosslyn the pillars generate the various Reshel patterns that contain the basic etheric vaults. The vaults contain the seeds for manifestation of the spiritual energies into the physical realm.

Since the pillars at Rosslyn Chapel lock into the vaults by their mathematical spacing and corresponding angles created that accord with the Reshel, when light workers use the system their spiritual work is heightened considerably. The geometry is an expression of the higher divine will as gleaned by man in inner work such as the light work described earlier. According to the spiritual intent of the practitioner the different modes are used to link with one another at different levels.

The Golden-Ratio Rhombus
The Golden Section is a term applied to a line divided in the proportion of 1:1.618 (a ratio known as the Golden Ratio), from which stems the Golden Spiral, a growth pattern present in many life forms. 1.618 is also known as the Phi ratio. In short, Phi supports and generates life in many forms. An L with the

two arms drawn in this ratio to one another can then be pivoted in the four cardinal directions to make a kite shape known as the Golden Ratio rhombus, or simply the Golden Rhombus (see **Figure 5**).

Whenever you have a basic Reshel form there are rhombuses present also, since they function together. Their symbiotic relationship is discussed later.

The rhombic mechanism is a higher function or stage of the Reshel, and is an expression of a superior state of being that becomes a universal communications system with various functions, managing or supporting or creating gates, pillars (light tubes), and primary manifesting systems. It can also use complex energy systems to interact with specialized dynamics such as the Grail energy system. The various functions were determined from using the format in group light process. It is the ideal form of light chariot or *merkabah*.

Within the rhombus there are both short and more elongated versions of the basic form. The apex of the 2.618 (the phi number squared) rhombus is known as the Kronos point and is a low frequency Time Gate. The apex of the 1.618 rhombus is known as the Tsadey or Glory Pole and is a high frequency Time Gate. The two are complementary in the same system.

A Time Gate is not meant to convey the notion of a space ship in time travel; this expression relates to inner states whereby you can access real time. There are spiritual requisites that, once fulfilled, will allow the process to unfurl. A relatively pure state of grace and right intent allows one to access all realms and dimensions for the sake of common good and highest service to the divine light beings under the Christ energy. Anything less will not open the gates, and any attempt is highly dangerous if unsupervised, since this is specialist light work and previously was secret knowledge applied by highly specialized groups. It is possible to physically transport via these gates but this is not suggested here as a safe procedure and is not for experimentation.

The rhombus uses an L shape as its abbreviated form that can be incorporated into temples and earth grids as well as human light bodies. The basic L is portrayed in the ancient letter "Gamele" in proto-Sinaitic. Other Hebrew letters also incorporate the L principle in their designs. For ease of recognition here, only the top right L is depicted, though there are three other Ls inherent in the rhombus depending on the polar requirements in the process. See **Figure 5**.

When two rhombuses are placed adjacent and offset to one another a new rhombus is formed where they overlap, and a new Resh point is formed where the horizontal lines of the original L shapes intersect. This Resh point will be found at Point A, a little way back from the horizontal ends of the original single Ls. See **Figure 6**.

There is an L that feeds into Rosslyn in **Figure 7**, showing Rosslyn at the A point in **Figure 6** so that it is placed at the centre of two offset or overlapping rhombuses, with the horizontal lines of the Golden Ls overlapping on Rosslyn. The L in the landscape is marked approximately by Inchcolm Island, Black Hill in the Pentlands where a Sinclair tower once stood, and Rosslyn Chapel. The Resh point in this L would be the hinge point of the L in Black Hill. See **Figure 7**.

The rhombuses, like other light mechanisms, can shrink or expand continuously to do various tasks at any one time, and even rotate and spin on their axes, and duplicate temporarily. Using another Golden Ration Rhombus, and setting it within the context of the local landscape around Rosslyn, the Rose Line coincides with its central axis. See **Figure 8**.
The Rose Line also lies on the central axis of the local basic Reshel Third Breastplate matrix, so the points labelled mark

various poles set within the primary Reshel pattern, and the rhombus drawn in **Figure 8** is overlaying this system as a higher subsystem of light codes. Arthur's Seat, the peak hill in Holyrood Park is also set on the Rose Line, and there are a number of significant leys that traverse this area. Arthur's Seat in the Tsadey pole is in effect the generating/ seeding or Christos pole for the Reshel in **Figure 8**, with the Rosslyn Resh pole being equivalent to the Goddess/*Shekinah*. There are often two poles set either end of a ley line or section of it that perform different functions, and the energies can flash between the poles reversing the direction of flow up or down the line. In a higher reality the energy is traveling in both directions, but often in normal reality it might be perceived as a one-way flow. Setting the poles graphically for a one way flow allows an ease of recognition. The two poles are called dipoles. At times sensitive dowsers can pick up this alternative flow of energy as they are tapping into the higher Metatronic realm where things are reversed. Leys with Metatronic alignment exhibit these phenomena which are due to a principle called the Flashing Dynamic, whereby all is continually in a flux as the etheric poles exchange their energies and interpenetrate.

Having looked at the simplest and most local matrix of Reshel patterns that incorporate the Rose Line, it must be added that the Rose Line begins in Orkney, passes through Thurso and down through Rosslyn and Glastonbury and ends near Hendaye (near the holy mountain of San Sebastian in the Pyrenees).

William Buehler has done a fascinating Reshel analysis of the coat of arms of the Sinclairs that he calls the Shamir Arms whereby he incorporates the Bird-Serpent Staff of Aesculapius into the Rose Line, so the ley line becomes the staff with the eye of the shamir or serpent at Thurso. This can be viewed at: http://www.shameer-orion.org/pdf/HenrySinclairArms01.pdf
As a whole it describes the process of regeneration or second

birth and hints at the special role the Sinclairs played in relation to the Christ figure. The bird at the crown would relate to the cockerel in Sinclair heraldry, which links with the brood hen and its twelve chicks. "Linn" translates as the hen and the Lyn/linn includes the meaning as the brood of twelve. "Ros" is the Rose. The Rose Line can be seen as a line with the Zodiacal signs placed along it. It is also represented in the Grail as the twelve knights. Later we will look at the 12/13 dynamic which is all important for the Ascension process.

The Resh

When applied to the local landscape, the upper Resh pole is set at Rosslyn. Its complementary pole is the Shiyn. While the Resh is vital and synthesizes part of the Reshel, the Shiyn pole (in this instance at Mount Lothian on the Rose Line) is the pole which is chiefly concerned with synthesizing all the nodes or poles in the geometry. However, there is no functioning chapel anymore at Mount Lothian, so Rosslyn which lies in the complementary pole is in the next best control point for the Reshel here. Within Judaeo-Christian mysteries the Resh was known as the Chief Headstone of God, and its position in the geometry of the Reshel triangle lies at 26 degrees 18 minutes from the base line of the triangle, a special angle known as the Bethlehem angle due to the angle made from the line of latitude at the Great Pyramids to the position of Bethlehem. (It is created by the angle formed when drawing a diagonal line within a 2:1 rectangle.) The Bethlehem angle can also be called the Grail angle as it leads within the Great Pyramid into the Resh pole that establishes the apex or "Great Step", the 29th Step in the 28-steps leading into the Grand Gallery where initiations took place. This ascent uses the same 26.3 degree angle.

Buehler is convinced that the Sinclairs incorporated the sacred angle of 26 degrees 18 minutes into their engrailed cup — the eight Grail cups in each direction on the cross have used this angle according to Buehler, but extant versions of the cross vary. The engrailed cup is designed to carry Christ's blood or other forms of similar elixir, and the angle deployed takes account of his birthplace! See **Figure 9**.

In summary, the Reshel system uses the Grail angle to locate the vital Resh pole which determines the creation and placement of the parabolic Grail crescent. The Resh pole lies at the center of the elixir filling the cup, and at a higher level drives a tube that connects with the Shiyn pole. The pillar connecting the two poles generates new life forms and is known as the Layooesh or Zoii pillar in esoteric terminology.
Within the landscape (see **Figure 8**) the Shiyn and Zayin poles hold no functioning temples or artifacts any longer-the Zayin the north is at Seafield Tower that the Sinclairs used to control, while the Zayin in the south is at Dryburgh Tower (now renovated for private use). However, there are two major bodies of water nearby in each case; Kinghorn Loch and St Mary's Loch respectively so this will allow the memory of the land to be stored effectively since water holds memory.

In terms of the Sinclair cup design Rosslyn at the Resh pole becomes the Grail part of the whole Reshel system, being linked to the only effective control position within the geometry! In these times blood relations are not as significant though, and Buehler often uses a term "paragenetic Sinclair" to describe those who are integrating the Reshel into their spirituality.

The ancient Hebrew letter for Resh is a side view of a head, and the head was venerated thus by the Knights Templar who were working intimately with the Reshel. Within mythology, the dynamic of Gawain and the Green Knight expresses the earth's qualities and its recurring energetics or energy processes at Rosslyn. Gawain was charged with beheading the Green Knight who in turn never died. The head being the Resh, the symbolism of the story is paramount.

Above all the Resh and other symbols used in the Reshel geometry are states of consciousness. Buehler says:

One example is in Psalm 118:19-22 which describes both the Resh and the L-gates (the L uses two complementary systems). In this passage the L becomes the corner head stone or corner Resh. There are two gates – one of righteousness and the main one of the Lord/Yahwey. The stone that the builder rejected (real meaning "made hollow, so becoming the Selah or Unmanifest God essence") is to become the head-stone of the corner.

Open to me the gates of the righteousness: I will go into them, and I will praise the Lord:

This gate of the Lord, into which the righteous shall enter.

I will praise thee: for thou hast heard me, and art become my salvation.

The stone (in) which the builders enclosed the Nothingness is become the head stone of the corner. Psalms 118:19-22 King James version

Of course the words have to be back traced to Hebrew and then the metaphysical meanings used... and understood".

Within the chapel layout, the lower chapel forms one of the two L's (Gates of Righteousness) in the Christic Reshel. The same appears in the Chartres' St. Piat chapel, Montserrat basilica and in other cathedrals, where incidentally Black Madonnas are on display - it is highly likely there once was one at Rosslyn too. See **Fig 10**.

A small sacristy has been added onto the earlier lower chapel. The position and size of this sacristy fits exactly with the L geometry of the Christic half of the Reshel at Rosslyn. The recently built wooden shelves there carried a number of rejected carvings; the figure of Judas clutching a money bag was on display at the peak of the L. where the Christie Resh pole resides. After I identified it the stone mysteriously disappeared in May 2006. Symbolically, it was appropriate for Judas to have

found his way here. The name Judas is synonymous with the Yuda or Yud letter, and the temporary placing of him in the crucial spot, albeit unconsciously, was a manifestation that the Yud light codes were being inserted by the angelic hierarchies.
Its presence on the spot would have served as a temporary etheric installation of foundational fire into the Christos Headstone (Resh) point. (A later section will focus on the Judas dynamic.)

The L Mechanism in the Chapel
The chapel can be operated using the L mechanism alongside others in order to enter into its divine essence. When using the L, or rhombus, in conjunction with Rosslyn Chapel, the initiate was going directly to the "hot spots" without necessarily passing through the normal series of stations laid down in the chapel. Correct use of the L by skilled light workers will translate the temple into a true no-time/ all-time (also called non-linear Time) mode from which valid work may be done in a past, present and future time continua with Metatronic agencies who work under the mandate of the archangel Michael.

Buehler says: "The bypassing of all stations demands the pure God Essence or Selah (Rest, Silence), clarity of the operator holding the position and the ones transiting the Bay and station of the Chief Head Stone conditioned by the codes of the angels there. This marks a major "L-Shift" at this point which effectively brings the Unmanifest divine Essence into manifestation as the Manifest God / "God of Peace".

This is referred to in the original Hebrew in the New Testament and translated as the "Peace of God" in Phil. 4:7
And the peace of God, which passeth all understanding, shall keep your hearts and minds through Jesus Christ
And in Phil 4:9
Those things which ye have both learned, and received, and heard, and seen in me, do; and the God of peace shall be with you.

This tells us of polarity at the highest state: the "God of Peace" and "Peace of God" (Phil 4:7-9) which bracket the 8-point (listed qualities) of a star-tetrahedron. "Peace" relates to the Rest or Selah State. The Selah exists beyond Mind or "understanding." This passage will render many other lessons in male and female polar interaction.

The L shift is the most vital, critical single movement in the whole Chapel's activation within light work. Rosslyn is the chapel that brings about peace through its intricate and actively encoded light network. The carvings are merely signifying this – the real action lies in the hearts of men. As a former minister at the chapel would say to visitors; "You are mistaken if you come to worship these stones, but please find and worship the Christ within you".

The L, then, is a shorthand version of the full Golden Ratio Rhombus. It is known esoterically as the *Eye of Ra*, and compliments the Third Breastplate of Metatron also known the Eye of Isis. Thoth says:

> "The Isis Eye is the **Star Gate** into the *Attasic* or complete Universe. This is the Eye of reconciliation with the *Eye of Ra*. Once the Isis Eye is wedded with the *Eye of Ra*, the latter is returned to Source"

Essentially the Golden Rhombus is at the core of the interchange between Spirit and Matter, and so is involved in manifesting Spirit. There are a number of time apertures along the *Event Horizon* that are managed by the *Eye of Ra* via a number of holes created for the various stages of manifestation to pass through. When it is fully functioning there will be a free ebbing and flowing of energies from the higher Universes and harmony will be restored.

When the L is operative as a light mechanism, realities from radically different realms temporarily unite. There are always various stages of reality in existence at one moment; the reality normally perceived is only one of mundane possibilities. When one is an aware individual other planes of existence are perceived automatically. In light work the dynamic of a flashing universe encompasses these various planes of reality and is at play. Its three primary states are as follows (see **Figure 4**) :

Compression of Mind

This uses the five platonic solids as a grid frame and is the universe we are generally accustomed to.

Light

This is shaped like a torus or imploded sphere – when we pull the manifested form inside out we create a torus. It alternates with the manifested form and is more real but not as real as the final state

Neutra

The universe is neither in the light nor manifested by mind, so is represented by the Great Void or Selah.

Since Rosslyn is very much concerned with the various planes of reality, the important right-angled dynamic known as the **L move** is woven into the layout of the chapel and connects with many of the subsystems in the chapel. You could say that the chapel resembles a computer in which Metatronic software programs are downloaded so the computer is continually upgraded to adapt to the demands placed upon it when interfacing with the world.

The L is the centre of the golden rhombus as discussed, and signifies a change of frequency. Interestingly, the knight's move in chess could well be a representation of the shift in consciousness required to access deeper soul levels or higher dimensions of light. Physiologically we have L moves in our heart region and pineal gland that seem to affect how we feel and perceive respectively.

Focusing on the ground plan of the chapel, we can trace one right angle where a line or path leads along the main pillars at the edge of the Lady Chapel, and then turns ninety degrees at the Apprentice Pillar marked by the serpents, to descend to the lower chapel. The line not only turns ninety degrees – it turns from the horizontal plane and descends vertically, rather like the movement of a serpent. This shift follows the shape of the Nun letter, and the path continues in the lower chapel to make a second right angled turn when the line turns from the main axis of the lower chapel and goes into the small sacristy to the left hand side. This sacristy hosts the Christic Resh pole as described earlier.

When we pause on the line after it has turned ninety degrees from the Apprentice pillar, we are on the wider step leading down to the lower chapel at Rosslyn, in line with the central bosses on the Rose Line in the Lady Chapel. At this point, we may assimilate the energies met in the chapel above (in particular the high light codes held at the Ulta point and those generated by the 8 point wheel from the Mari pillar (seen in **Figure 17**).

Chapter Three: Examples of the Poles and their Functions in the Chapel

The Alpha Pole

Rosslyn is the apex module in all the several Reshel grids covering Europe, on into the Middle East grounding at Mt. Sinai. ..... Rosslyn has had installed the planetary Christic Alpha Pole downloaded from the Schiehallion/Fortingall line into the Edinburgh Matrix (Rosslyn controlling). It polarizes with another rod at Glastonbury. All this power and function uploads into Rosslyn via its central "Ulta" pole.

The Ulta Pole (also known as Zion or Zayin pole)

This pole accepts and sorts out this vastly complicated signal, distributing the thousands of vectors through the Reshel sub systems. The *Ulta pole* is located on the East wall, under the rose window in the Lady Chapel, on the chapel's centre line. It is near the wall in the N-S line through the four altars on that wall. The *Ulta pole* is too holy to have an altar and should not be approached when the Chapel is fully "online".

The *Ulta pole* is really where the path of the Reshel begins. It is supported by two generating poles that lie outside the chapel in its grounds, and as such it lies within two overlapping rhombuses – this in effect places the Chief Head Stone of God or the Resh (Hebrew) within its domain. (It is important to realize when studying Buehler's diagrams that there are a number of positions in the chapel which pinpoint the Resh pole according to which Reshel subsystem we are working with.)

We note in the Reshel ground plan that most of the Christos' half of the grid is not in the chapel but is outside, to the East. The purpose and result of this is to keep persons out of this area. Most grids present the *Shekinah*, female system to interact with. The female is the Generator in basic male-female polar interchange. Her composite pattern is difficult to operate but once mastered new levels can be attained. If the female part of the grid can be cleared and become functional, the male part will activate. In recognizing the special qualities and functions of the *Shekinah* or "Goddess" many temples will have the "Lady Chapel" as a distinct area and in the East. When the two halves of the chapel grid are interacting, there are two vital parts of the Christos' half that are inside the building: the most holy altar (Christos Resh pole) and the L-Gate system.

Continuing now with more detail, we trace the central axis beyond the *Ulta pole* and reach the side sacristy to the lower chapel, which was added as an apparent inner sanctum at the time the upper or main chapel was built, the main part of the lower chapel being at the very least one hundred years older. Two large rhombuses overlap in this tiny side room at a very holy Resh point, where the high priest would have prepared for service. This room would also keep relics and various other sacramental objects too holy to have accessed by anyone other than a qualified priest.

The most sacred Christic altar is in this room; it is the Resh in the Christic half of the Reshel so is known as the Christic Resh (as opposed to the *Shekinah*/Christ's Bride Resh). Rosslyn Chapel is set at the centre of two overlapping rhombuses within a forty mile radius in the landscape, and this dynamic is paralleled in miniature in the small side room below (see **Figure 10**).

In the layout of the chapel the Ulta point in the Lady Chapel is uniquely placed to bridge both halves of the basic Reshel – the female and male halves come together here (see **Figure 3**) – these are apices of downward and upward pointing Gizeh type pyramids (or aeriopaxes). In effect the Ulta point here in the chapel controls a much wider Reshel grid spinner in the landscape than whatever is generated in the microcosmic geometry of the chapel itself.

It is also the uppermost tip of a large etheric pentagram oriented along the central axis. This point allows access into the higher forms of the Reshel and its associated higher realities within the wider universe. This holy center can only be approached through the female stations of the temple.

The *Ulta pole* is so sacred it is not used and instead there is another spot on the wide step below that allows the initiate access to the Ulta point. The step affords safe access for humans to interface with the Ulta, and is firmly placed within an area where the void or silence resides. Perhaps that is why above the Ulta point or pole (see **Figure 3**) in the Lady Chapel the delicately carved Green Man grins down, almost mockingly. He knows that the Ulta point itself cannot be accessed by humans.

My earlier book, The Spiritual Meaning of Rosslyn's Carvings describes a journey around the upper chapel which ends at the threshold to the stairs to the lower chapel, where the only writing in the chapel is placed on the lintel over the stairway. The wide landing on the stairs is placed on the Rose Line, in line with its central bosses of the Lady Chapel slightly above. It is here rather than on the Ulta point that you can safely pause to assimilate the mechanisms of the upper chapel, and reflect and renew the connections.

The *Ulta pole* (Centre) spins the primary Reshel system from within the Lady Chapel, and it also sets up a secondary eight point spinner at the Mari Pillar, this spinner acting as a subsystem or "rider" for the main system. The higher forms of the Reshel are accessed at the Ulta/Zion pole in the chapel. This is the ninth and final station in the chapel lying just before the central pillar on the East wall (where it generates an etheric form known as the Penta Dove which is matched in the physical on the external wall in a carving of the same!).

The Nine Internal Poles

Although there are physical stations for the initiate to pass through in the chapel, it is important to realize that by doing so they are embracing an internal system of poles with etheric functions. There are nine internal poles within the Reshel system that correlate with the Ennead, a Seraphimic grouping of archai overseeing the present time continuum. The "Michael Mandate" comes under the Ennead group; simply put: the archangel Michael administers Ennead directives.

The nine-fold Ennead was the focus of one of the chapters in my book *The Spiritual Meaning of Rosslyn's Carvings.*. The Onata are high spiritual mediating beings within the Metatronic realms that communicate with the Elisaphane of the Oritronic fallen realms. Communications systems are under the oversight of the Ennead and of Michael who maintain safe mechanisms for the exchange between the realms to take place. The nine internal poles of the Reshel are grouped into four poles, three poles and two single poles as systems in the following way:
Tsadey at the apex of the Great Pyramid dynamic contains a four pole system concerned with the process of manifestation (these poles being the Shiyn, Teyth, Dallet and Tsadey); the Star of David is essentially a three pole system for making connections (these poles being the Vau, Yud and Beth), the Zayin pole as the 8th pole lies at the apex of the pentagram that represents the five Onata seeding energies in the Elisaphane exchange. The Resh as the ninth pole unifies it all.

The Resh, ninth pole also generates the Grail cup further correlating with Lunar dynamics (seen as a Crescent Moon) and a Creation Field (bulls' horns). In the advanced geometry of the Grail a primary plane of Metatronic reality is established in the Neutra Universe. (That plane is a "teleplane" which establishes the action in a temporal state.) Two Resh poles are created equidistant from the plane, these two marking the beginning of the Metatronic Reshel system. These poles are loaded with the state of being and consciousness needed to generate the reality objectives in the basic plane. The synergic unity of the Plane and two specialized (male, female) Reshel then creates a cosmic "antenna" capable of scanning all dimensions and Time continua for the type of systems needed for the project at hand. This cosmic dish-antenna is the Grail Cup, constructed as a parabolic curve spun into a dish form and integrated into the Reshel system with several actions. The main point is that the Resh pole is the transmitting and receiving node, working with the Dish and basic plane in the Neutra Universe.

When the Resh poles are merged in the *Ulta Pole* (the Center of the whole system) the cups are joined on their "rims" (See **Figure 11**) which is the basic process for generating a core system of resolution known as the Aphatheta system within an Ark creation, as well as being in the center of the Aeriopax. The Aeriopax is another name for a special Reshel system used to facilitate the "Ascension" or "Transition", This merging of the Resh poles forms a 9-pole "Vault of the Corpus" also called the "Eye of God" in advanced Ark applications. The archetypal symbol includes a bird or anything with two heads, or a head with 2 faces, or the double-stone, split stone, split or double mountain, or split head. The open area in the split or between the two faces relates to the Selah Field where creation begins, or the *Ulta Point..*

Figure 11 shows the Resh poles slightly separated but this is done so that the central *Ulta pole* can be shown. Usually that is not perceived by persons or shown in grids unless special work is being linked into the Neutra Universe, as with the Ark Applications for example.

The series of physical stations in the chapel lie along the central axis and culminate on the Star of David over the altar. Two of the stations lie outside the main chapel just beyond its door and serve to link the site of the old chapel in the cemetery below with the current one. William Buehler explains that there are a series of stations for the initiate to pass through that reflect the geometry of the Reshel.

The Vau Pole

The Vau pole as a Hebrew letter is number 6 (see **Figure 12**), and is at the apex of the six-sided figure commonly known as the Star of David. The Vau Pole has already been mentioned in relating the Beyth./ Nun Yud dynamic, and is positioned where the Mari pillar stands behind the altar. When we stand at the Vau pole we are to become like a new pillar. The Vau stands at the apex of an equilateral triangle which creates a tetrahedron. Thoth says: "The tetrahedron serves as the first pillar in the spiritual temple and is a vehicle of higher Light manifestation into the matter plane.....It serves as the connection between that which is envisioned and that which is accomplished. Its power flow is from above (the zenith) to below (the nadir), through the three Divine Creation Signals or Tetramorphs, which are a trinity of Elohim command posts stationed with the greater geometric crystalline matrices of the universal domain". (I believe that these Elohim command posts are represented by the three carved pyramids in the line of five pinnacles above the east wall of the Lady Chapel, and the Elohim work in conjunction with the Yaveh format to create the polarities we see in the nature kingdom and our human world.) This Pillar and Temple is found in Revelation 3:7-13; the Key of David is the 6-pointed star and related star-tetrahedron. However the "Temple" is part of what modern mystics call the "Layooesh Pillar" wherein the star-tetrahedron function is supplemented by the star-pentahedron (interpenetrated Pyramids) and augmented by a 12-point wheel. This system is formed in the routine Reshel interaction.

The Tsadey Pole

This is the sixth station in a series that activates the Chapel's primary Reshel system, and is also known as the Glory Pole.

From the Tsadey pole the chapel's codes spiral out in Golden Ratio spirals to ground in the "Pools of Shiyn/Life/the Moon" on either end of the *event horizon* on the east wall (this sets up a harmonic with the two moons that originally orbited Earth as mentioned by Rudolf Steiner and Thoth/Rev Maia). The higher number stations were accessed from the Glory pole without having to actually move there physically. The higher initiate has to engage here with the fire codes generated from the Central Sun of all Central Suns according to Buehler, as the appropriate response to the outpouring energies of the Ennead. This Central Sun is the unfallen star "Mazuriel", representing the Sacred Heart (Manifest); Denebola in Leo is in the place of the star in our present universe. The Templars used that position when constructing stellar grids; a dramatic example is its use at Mont St. Michel relative to the Virgo grid in France formed by Chartres and other Marian cathedrals.

Chapter Four: The Lady Chapel

The Shekinah

The Lady Chapel is a clear dedication to the *Shekinah*, Goddess or Lady of Light, a motif that is connected to the Beyth pole. The meanings of the *shekinah* include a lodging, or container for forms to exist in, an ark, and a 4 square reality frame or vault. The Beyth is drawn as a square or dwelling place or ark. It is wise to remember that all physical Arcane systems like vaults and pyramids are outer manifestations of inner energetic thought systems. The Lady Chapel becomes the SHEKINAH MARI or the Dwelling of Mari.

Mari in turn is linked to the womb of creation in the upper chapel. Her name means "bitter distillation" but more importantly: "vision, mirror." The 2-sided mirror is a model of a "teleplane" or Time Continuum system. (The ancient language used "Mar" as water that designates a continuum system.) The Lady Chapel or dwelling place is liberally adorned with cubes on her arches – there are 215 of them, which is one less that 216 – a number that some Hebrew scholars interpret as a holy number, being a hidden reference to the creator. . 215 gives the word: "H'Yar: the reverent, flow of water, shooting an arrow, teaching," The flow of water (stream, waterfall) relates to the lin/linne meanings in a temporal context and the projection of an arrow transfers codes from one system to another as well as the reverse path of the arrow (also the act of teaching). The "codes" are engrammed in the stone with outer symbols relating to them.

The essence of the cube as the creator and its own dwelling place as Beyth shares an intimate relationship with the *Shekinah/* goddess that cannot be over-emphasized in relation to Rosslyn. At the Mari pillar there is also an intimate connection between the Vau pole (discussed in later section) and the Lady Chapel behind her, based on the spiritual light codes of ancient Hebrew.

There needs to be a void or emptiness in which things are created, called the "Selah" in Hebrew. Selah means "the suspension point, fulcrum of scales, silence between musical notes." This represents the Unmanifest God and source of Life. The design of the chapel allows this; parallel to the Rose Line running along the north–south axis in the Lady Chapel there is another internal chapel line on the east wall that represents the Selah, contained in the number 58. Buehler also saw a physical vision of the number 58 in the actual full moon. (This number remained in his view for about 20 minutes.) The number has also appeared in Templar lore as 1058, engraved on a silver head of a woman. The number 58 translates as "Noach (misnamed "Noah" in scripture) meaning "Silence, Rest", that is, the vital Selah Essence of God and source of life. However when the number is viewed in the opposite direction its "chen" meaning "Grace, love." The Templars understood this, also that "Chen" has three spellings, the other meanings relating to the Pillar connective and to Form as the vineyard or pedestal foundation. When one version is used, all three are implied. The "Chen" is also found in the name "Enoch (Chenowk)" and relates to the Enochian mysteries. When Genesis 1-9 is analyzed we find Enoch as the Sephira Tiphereth in the Cabalist Tree, the Messianic correspondence, with Noach generating the Ark and Form. The Templars added "1000, master number of Aleph, #1 giving the 58 a system for creating an ARK ... this is an advanced Reshel science beyond the scope of this book. When I was in Jordan with the Bedhouins I saw the numbers 1058 in a vision without realizing their meaning at the time. (At the time of writing there is an investigation into the distinct probability that Rosslyn is forming a Metatronic Ark system.)

There are many names for this line that in effect divides the Selah or Sacred Void within two etheric planes called teleplanes, out of which reality is spun. One of its names is the Horizon of Thoth. This is an *event Horizon* (see **Figure 1 and 19),** and it has two surfaces similar to the two sided mirror (which could well be the true meaning of the Pictish mirror sign, since the Reshel can be found in other ancient codes too). As noted above, in Hebrew the word "mar" refers to this creation vault, and the word is of course found within "Mari" to whom this chapel is dedicated, as are many other Templar Marian cathedrals. Essentially this line along the east wall contains the reality codes for whatever is being created in the Chapel. It has two primary overall codes: the CHRISTIC which is emphasized in the lower chapel, and the *Shekinah* which resides in the main chapel above.

Beyth and Nun: A Greasing Process

Please refer to these letters in the attached graphic—see **Figure 12**. There is a complex overlay of ongoing spiritual processes at play in the chapel so this esoteric guide cannot cover the processes in depth. I personally am attracted to the two letters Beyth and Nun, and how they combine in the plan of the chapel. Beyth (as is the Yud in the complimentary pole) is positioned at the Threshold of Sythia and taking into consideration the proximity of the *Ulta Pole* in the chapel it works with its counter pole the Yud. In the following exploration I am looking at another dynamic though, where Beyth and Yud seem to dovetail and augment their individual meanings into a composite or synergic whole, as an example of how the chapel arranges its parts to harmonize. Beyth is drawn as a square with a door in the southeast and Nun is drawn as two right angled steps going from top left to bottom right (a southeast direction). In essence, merging the letters Nun and Beyth allows the process of initiation to run more smoothly as these two letters then connect with the Vau pole. Beyth also works closely with Nun to link the *Ulta pole* to the wide step on the stairway where humans can interface in a safe mode with the extremely high energies.

Focusing first on Nun, the steps in the chapel are in the southeast, leading from where the Apprentice pillar stands. From the Apprentice pillar we make the two right angled moves by first turning at a right angle from the horizontal plane on which the Rose Line lies to the vertical plane at which the steps descend, in accordance with the Nun letter. The second section of the Nun letter is marked by the small sanctuary off at a right angle to the left in the room below-the area that, as we have seen, holds the Christic Head Stone or Christic Resh. This stepping of Ls or right angles in order to reach a room below is echoed in St Piat's Chapel in Chartres Cathedral in France.

Non or Nun, number 50 is often described as the serpent letter Shamir in ancient Hebrew. "Shemir" translates as "a thorn, diamond, keenness for scratching or penetration, to hedge with thorns (crown of thorns), guard or protect, observe, preserve, settlings of wine." As the word combination: "Shem-iyr" we would have meanings: "shem: honor, authority, name, hear, obey, sound" and "iyr: a city, watcher as an angel, open the eyes, awaken" or spelled differently:" "Nun" translates as "resprout, be perpetual, propagate by shoots." This provides the idea of perpetual life typified in plant repropagation.

Thoth describes the Shamir:
>   The worm will bore into the center of the Tree of Life and Light will pour out as if from a Golden Wound into the center of every heart."

In every pillar, tower, tree, etc. there is a "gap" or Neutra Universe state which will generate the vertical and horizontal components: the central pillar and the teleplane supporting the Form. This Gap has pure unpolarized Life which is foundational to a creation realm of unpolarized "White Selah" and what might be called "Life Fire" or in Hebrew the "Chor" fire (white, pure, fire). The Sham-iyr is an interface system for awakening,via a threefold action creating the Gap, generating the Tree (or tower, pillar) and creating the round ring or "city" to contain the Form.

In the Eden Tree the Serpent (Shamiyr) passed the fruit to Chavah (Eve) also meaning life, so there is a 3-phase transference of Life from the Tree of Life, through the Shamiyr, to the woman "chay, or chavah."

Where do we see serpents but at the base of the Apprentice Pillar! This pillar is an intrinsic part of the Nun dynamic in the chapel! Perhaps the letter Nun best sums up Rosslyn – it translates as **eternal regeneration**. Certainly as mentioned earlier, among other vital functions Rosslyn is a **Serpent or Dragon Temple**. More orthodox Christian theology denigrated the snake as something evil, but its true status in spiritual terms is a vital one for understanding the Christ energy of integration and fluidity. Serpents or snakes were revered in ancient cultures for their ability to shed their skins and live anew in the flesh. The shedding skin represents a spiral or cyclic regeneration or "re-sprouting" as still found in the Hebrew translation. The Reshel light codes are chiefly concerned with the process of constant regeneration, so the whole language of the sacred geometry has a close affinity with this letter. There are eight snakes or shamir or serpents or dragons at the base of the pillar, representing the letter Nun in the Tree of Life of Raa and Towb in the Centre of Eden. From their mouths they generate the eternal greenery in the chapel, and also generate metaphysically the codes for creation and the True Vine that empowers all of Rosslyn. (The pillar also carries the Elemental or Devic codes in which the Chapel specializes. Devic and animal realms represent the Nature races which are also involved in the synergy of light programs for Earth to enter the Full Light spectrum.) The Dragon/Serpent dynamic can be viewed in addition as the river North Esk in the landscape outside (water is a key element in storing our feminine earth wisdom).

Beyth as a letter is affiliated in a highly spiritual etheric form with a particular cube function within a star-tetrahedron which has 8 points; connecting the points also gives you a cube. The Lady Chapel is adorned with cubes. When you view the X crosses that adorn the cubes, you might imagine that using the cube as a cross provides manifesting ability. The Star of David itself is centred on the Vau pole above the Lady Chapel. Moreover, in light group processing with Buehler's group, the word Non or Nun was linked with Sanctuary, and an original word for God. The Nun became a cube within the star tetrahedron (three-dimensional six pointed star). Since Beyth is closely associated with the cube as a geometric form, the link between the two letters can be noted here. Beyth exists to fully engage with any system so the light codes will actually ground themselves. Beyth as a dwelling place is providing the best foundation for life to regenerate in all realms of existence.

To summarize, the Lady Chapel can be seen as a Beyth letter or formation with the Apprentice pillar positioned in its southeast doorway, the pillar providing a pivotal point in the multi-dimensional portal at Rosslyn. The cubes too can be viewed as mini-Beyths, that are augmented by their location in the chapel. Beyth supports the chapel to go past the point of no return so that all regenerative forms of life can be supported. This alone would make for the ultimate Green Chapel! Buehler explains that the Beyth and the Nun are in close cohort then; the Beyth being the form and the Nun the mechanism for it to appear.

Thoth says that the Nun letter on a microcosmic scale lies within the origins of DNA as a "generative wave form". It appears that the makers of Rosslyn were concerned with new life forms down to a microscopic scale, and Buehler has been trying to decode the proto-Sinaitic light codes in the Old Testament to determine what creates life and new DNA strands.

Before we go into greater depth showing how the nodes of the Reshel interweave and interconnect, we can glance upwards to view the main window above the Mari Pillar/Vau Pole. When we feed the Beyth/ Nun dynamic into the Vau (6) pole we are essentially creating a new earth star.

Beyth is an ark, and Vau in turn supports it in the form of a pillar that is the "Pillar in the Temple of God" as described in the Book of Revelation. (Revelation 3:7-12).

Chapter Five: The Central Window and its secret numbers or letters

Bill Buehler has interpreted the stonework tracery in the window (**Figure 13**) as a pattern of superimposed letters in the ancient Hebrew language, which was one of the original five languages of light emerging from the *Aloii* languages according to Thoth/Maia. The ancient Hebrew letters contained within the window design are chief components of the basic Reshel system. The letters are also linked to geometric nodes within the horizontal floor plan of the chapel, and the close relations between the letters deserve mention.

The Mari pillar lies slightly beyond the Tsadey pole, in the Vau pole. Letter Vau carries the essential Six vibration. The window can be viewed as an extension of the Vau pole since it is directly above it. As a six vibration its chief function is to connect and communicate.

Vau (number six) and Tsadey (number ninety) are intrinsically paired to form a "stem and blossom" pattern visible in the window tracery. The letters are graphically contained within a simple round flower on a central stem with side stems. The Tsadey pole lies just below the Vau Pole in the ground plan of the chapel, while in the tracery it is mirrored in the same position vertically. See **Figure 14** and **Figure 15**

The "stem and blossom" relief is a common feature on many Templar burial marker stones. The Tsadey is also known as the *Shekinah* or Glory pole, its letter resembling a Fleur de Lys. Appropriately, the Stuart Dynasty adopted this sign. It is an ancient sign that energetically is the sacred logo for the Egyptian god Thoth, the god of architecture (according to Rev Maia/ Thoth), and was also the symbol adopted by the Merovingian dynasty whose lineage some believe gave rise to the Stewarts in medieval times. This family held most ancient and secret knowledge within its ranks. Certainly many early masons still wished for a return of the Stewarts/Stuarts to the throne in Scotland.

The square part of the window pattern mirrors the letter Beyth or number 2, which normally as discussed has an open door in its southwest section.

The equal armed cross within the circle in the main window is number 9 or Teyth and this symbolizes the new vibration of the Christ energy. Teyth was portrayed in Ireland and Scotland on many early Christian tall stone crosses. It does not have a position in the ground plan in the chapel but according to Buehler acts as a sun wheel rotating over the altar and reaching from the Vau pole into the Tsadey pole.

The letter Thav is a simple equal armed cross, and is contained within the Teyth (see **figure 12**). Thav represents the process of individualization, as we learn to be fully conscious in the temporal world. Whereas the Fish (letter Dallet, #4) as a symbol is the soul's ability to work in a temporal frame, the Cross is the mechanism to transcend the continuum, or rise from the Waters of Time (letter Mem, # 40) usually symbolized as a Wilderness. This is interesting to contemplate in terms of Christ's life and mission.
The simple cross also represents the Earth, and in a higher reality we become one with Earth, unified in/as the Solar being. **Figure 15** shows a further aspect of these letters, showing the Sun Wheel combining with the Cross to create a new letter Teyth that describes a state correspondent to the "new earth star", which is a completely new state of being to which the Earth will be transformed following the Ascension. Most people relate this as a new Heaven and a new Earth.

Thoth says that all planets are etherically contained within the host sun in the real (Metatronic) universes. Only in this fallen

(Oritronic) universe, with the apparent loss of Grace, we have gravity and the suns can not hold their planets. Thus we hang out in orbit. Buehler explains that Suns are highly evolved sentient beings, the true "citizens of cosmos" that are a harmonic of all the Central Suns and the Central Sun of all Central Suns: MAZURIEL or the Sacred Heart, manifest.

This is quite a crucial concept. A "Central Sun" in a community of Suns is similar to a Messiah relative to humans. So Mazuriel would be a Messiah of all Messiahs. In this respect it can be better understood to represent it as the actual Sacred Heart of God since humans can understand that.

Taken as a whole, the window that towers above the Lady Chapel is proclaiming in code that all sentient levels of being on our planet Earth will undergo total transformation using the Christ energy and state of being. We see a new Earth Star in effect. The fact that it is a relatively modern window is irrelevant to the fact that this sacred intent has manifested in a form that is recognizable – it can be regarded as a Metatronic upgrade, just as the Baptistry added by the Victorians opened up the west wall and allowed people to enter over the Spirit to Matter pole (see **Figure 3**) when hitherto they entered by the north and south doors only. By stepping over this pole they will carry the light codes for this position at some level in their being. We must also adjust our thinking to understand that Time is non-linear and can be used both to create forms for future ages and for various stages of evolution in the interim.

Chapter Six: Examples of Reshel Dynamics

Buehler calls a square tower a "herm" after Thoth/Hermes who is the main Engineer-builder in the Hierarchy. Thoth was known as the god of architecture as well as of other sciences.

The Golden Bee

There was a natural beehive incorporated into a tower-like base to a pinnacle on the north end of the main gable containing the east window. In traditional spiritual knowledge there are two square towers or "Herms" that bracket the Omphalos or *hive shape* that centres any major energetic system. Where there is one tower on the Omphalos it would usually be a Herm. The correspondent pillar in the Lady Chapel has its square Herm with beehive in the northeast point of the eightfold wheel centred on the Mari pillar.

The Golden Bee is one of the two most important symbols of the **Solarian** beings (those beings that carry light codes from the solar frequencies in the Metatronic Realms**),** the other being a composite Holy Bird (primary ones used are the Eagle, Swan and Dove). As primary Solarian beings, they carry Solar codes that are inserted via the flower on the square tower. The significance of the bee is confirmed by the tonal frequency generated by the wings, probably a harmonic of the Continuum Frequency base known as the Flashing Universe (and heard by clients in the glen during a tour as a hum once!). The hexagonal comb cell is a harmonic of the Divine Heart connected to the Vau pole, and moreover honey is a form of elixir drawn from the Sun and plant pollen, which the bee transmutes. Moreover no bacteria can exist in honey, as if it were a foodstuff of the gods. The Gold of the honey is also resonant with the Golden Star Mazuriel. There are a several geometric mechanisms that facilitate access to the higher realms associated with Mazuriel.

The Star of David

The Star of David, shown in **Figure 16**, is centred on the present altar. When the initiate moves forward into the centre he enters the Tsadey (90) pole, also known as the *Shekinah*, or Glory pole. The scriptural reference to the basic Reshel First Breastplate of Metatron known as the Key of David is in Revelation 3:7-12. It refers to the Pillar in the Temple and the key to the door that no man can close or open – the Holy Grail dynamic in essence one could argue as it is so sacred it is illusive. Perhaps that is why the initiate remains in the centre of the Star of David and does not move beyond this point. The new Jerusalem and the new name of God are intrinsic to the process and are described in verse 12 of this mystery writing.

The six pointed star contains a two-way flow between matter and spirit. Vertically there is a central Matter–Spirit pole above the chapel here but in the vaults below there is the complementary Spirit-Matter pole. We carry the energy of the 6/Vau vibration horizontally along the central axis, where we encounter the penta dove in stone, at the very position that the Reshel pattern would dictate! This placing of the five doves just beyond the Ulta/Zayin pole of the upward pointing triangle is an expression of the sacred heart of God.

The Templa Mar

Above all the Vau is resonant with the Flower of Life and Sacred Heart of God. It infuses a strong Grace Factor into the proceedings. The Vau pole at the Mari pillar generates a vital eight-pointed wheel which can be used as the **Templa Mar** format that links in with the pillars. See **Figure 17**. The Templa Mar format is an eightfold etheric spinner, and can be seen on some of the early Masonic graves in the locality. The two outer pillars at the eastern end of the chapel are known as the Boaz or Master Mason's Pillar (the north east pole) and the Yahchen or Apprentice Pillar (the south east pole, also known as the Tree of Life**).** They are positioned on the **X cross** which

Yahchen or Apprentice Pillar (the south east pole, also known as the Tree of Life). They are positioned on the **X cross** which forms part of the geometry of the eight fold cross or wheel, which itself creates a spinner field far beyond the confines of the chapel. The Boaz pillar creates a needed harmonic with the Edinburgh system according to Buehler. It is the "Heel Stone" pole in the 8-point wheel and provides codes for both the cardinal and the diagonal (Saltire) crosses.

Buehler writes that in Solomon's Temple the Mason's Pillar was seen as Boaz and is the male Heel Stone that processes and then feeds spiritual seed-codes into the system while the Apprentice pillar acts like a female generator that provides the mechanisms for processing the seed codes it has received from Boaz. He notes that "Joachen" of Masonic tradition is better understood as "Yah-chen" or the Yah (Yud) that uses the three forms of "chen." These three spellings of the same word are found coded in Genesis and relate to the primary functions in creative process: forming the Pillar Connective, the Form(s) being connected, and the foundation of Grace. If one form of "chen" is used, all three are implied since they all are a synergic unity. This is why in the southeast we see many references to flowering and abundance in nature, essentially a female role. Many of the chapel's internal processes are facilitated by the dynamics of ancient Hebrew letters we have been describing, so carvings that bear relevance to these letters are placed in their appropriate places to mark the process at hand.

The Path of the Mother

The Mari (Vau) centre pillar is the point at which everything rotates within the Chapel's main manifesting system. It generates the Mari line that is one of the lines in the X cross, and as the Path of the Mother is aligned from northwest - southeast through the Eden tree (Apprentice Pillar which is the Tree of Life and Knowledge of Ra's and Towb) and onto the wide landing below the wall altar of Peter (Kaffa meaning light on why the serpents guard the tree at its base, as the Hebrew for serpent is Nun, meaning "regenerating life". When the initiate stands on the landing on the stairs they are required to assimilate the secrets of the Tree of Life and Knowledge before passing to the area below where the sequence leads them into the new higher form of Man. This directional path is also mentioned in my book *The Spiritual Meaning of Rosslyn's Carvings* in relation to the green women on the pinnacles in the southeast corner of the roof.

The Reshel system in the lower chapel arranges the Christic Boaz pillar and its L dynamics and is a major encoding system for the chapel as a whole. The Path of the Mother facilitates it. In the earth grids the Path of the Mother connects the east and west, or left and right brains of Europe and the Middle East.

Every system, whether stellar, planetary, or human, interconnects in the chapel to render its energies more efficient and focused for working with pure intent in light work.

Layooesh Pillar (Journeyman's Pillar)
The Layooesh Pillar is in the position that connects Heaven and Earth within the Kabbalah tradition. The pillar is seen to belong to the higher levels of Reshel dynamics and was mentioned in the section on the Resh earlier too. The Layooesh Pillar appears after a sequence of patterns is revealed in the Reshel light work process after the basic form (Key of David/Reshel Third Breastplate of Metatron) transmutes into a star tetrahedron, the Eye of God follows as an Ennead flash in the Tsadey pole and then a star pentahedron when two pyramids merge. The Layooesh is represented by the Journeyman's Pillar that is the central pillar of three bordering the Lady Chapel.

The Journeyman pillar has a "green skull" whose face closely resembles an ancient local powerful gypsy charm fashioned from a piece of coral. The coral type is known as the Brainstone since its patterning appears like DNA strands! This is aptly placed at this point in the Reshel where the DNA itself could be transformed. Mystics these days say that our DNA is undergoing rapid changes as we access the higher worlds with our rapidly increasing field of consciousness. Bill Buehler believes that the ancient Hebrew alphabet offers the codes to structure the future form of a 12 strand DNA, which will include its entire known letters and others not previously known to Man. Moreover, there is a thirteenth strand waiting in the wings to herald in the new continua, represented now by the unicorn/dolphin motifs.

The Three Pillars in Solomon's Temple in Creation Dynamics

The line of three pillars (master–journeyman–apprentice) represents the basic principles of creation. In Reshel dynamics, any two pillars when unified set up a field of creation and by default include a centre or central pillar as synthesis of the two pillars at the extremes. This is called a "Dion Couplet" with the central pillar resulting from a splitting of a stone or other object. For example, in the Hindi Maitri Upanishads 2.6 the Lord of Creation Prajapati cannot as One enter the pillar containing people so must become *five* breaths in order to create people, resulting in two vessels with life (agni) between them. Similarly in Genesis in the Old Testament the male and female levels (Zakar, Nequebah, Esh and Esha being male and female on two levels) become the dipoles setting up the *five* rivers and lands in Eden. Similarly in Irish mythology, Uisneach is the tree at the centre of the *five* provinces of ancient Ireland, and is intensely elemental in quality.

The splitting of images into two such as the two heads often facing opposite ways on early Masonic gravestones,   the double-edged sword and other phenomena all testify to the creation dynamics contained in the first five chapters of Genesis. There the silence or rest of Noach uses Nun (50) and

Cheyth (8) in one direction while the triple Grace factor of Chen in the other direction begets the three sons who are the Creation trinity. In the Lady Chapel behind the three pillars that set up the Dion Couplet there is the essential teleplane or Selah field from which all creation springs

Kaffa

Along the east wall there is an *event horizon* as mentioned earlier, and the high altar of Kaffa/Peter lies on it above the stairs. This altar correlates with the Chakra above the initiate's head when standing on the wide step on the stairs leading down beneath the altar. Kaf means "hollow stone", and its name infers a purity of intent that resonates with the name St Clair. In order to use the stone properly, its Selah (hollow or empty quality) must be understood, for the stonemason must fashion it from nothing and give it life. It can be engrammed with codes and I have successfully dowsed such stones, confirming my findings by comparison with Bill Buehler's Reshel analysis of the same stones.

The Grail King in effect was able to withdraw his sword from the stone because he could discern and use the Selah within the densest of matter, and the sword becomes the two poles within the one stone when the sword edges become mouths not edges. Peter or Simeon ben Yona recognized the state of being that generates creation when he uttered the name Messiah. In turn he received the name Hollow Stone or Kaffa for that is the foundation of all life within Form including thoughts and actions. The Kaf resides within all matter. The Kaffa altar here in Rosslyn acts as a form of gatekeeper to open the gate.

Kaffa can be seen as a gatekeeper, holding the key to advancing to higher levels, in which one has to be proficient within the Selah. Chapter I in the Gospel of St John 1:40-51 mentions the key disciples whom Yeshua charged with Christic mysteries that Thoth calls the Olgive charge, and the dynamics encoded show that Peter's brother Andrew forms a complementary pole with Peter. Nathaniel (Bartholomew) is important too and will be mentioned in terms of the Yud dynamic later.

There are twenty steps leading down, perhaps representing the twenty epochs of the earth the Mayans were aware of, or the twenty cycles in ascension that Thoth says Earth will undergo. In his commentary on the Sinclair shield Buehler shows that, when this is overlaid on the plan of the chapel the base of the cross lies at the Kaffa point on St Peter's Altar, and that the seventh step lies beneath it.
(This can be viewed at: http://www.shameer-orion.org/pdf/ SinclrShieldLChapel02.pdf)

20 is the number ascribed to the letter Kaf in Kaffa and meant "pure", "clear" in Hebrew–a word that resonates with St Clair. Originally Kaf was drawn as a crescent with two parallel lines beneath it, and was used in medieval heraldry by those familiar with the Reshel. This letter aligns well with the layout of the chapel where the Selah sandwich of two teleplanes is separated by the No-thing of Selah.

Kaf(fa) also contains the Aleph letter, depicted in Genesis 9:16-28 as the bow in the clouds. An important dynamic is presented here which keys into the Noah dynamic: the 350 year period during which Noah lived following the flood is a reference to the Shiyn in the centre of the Pools of Shiyn. This is found within the teleplane/waters of Mar in the Reshel, below the base of the triangle.

Noah is 58 in geomatria, the study of numbers that relate to the letters in ancient languages. In Hebrew, Noah means No-Thing, which forms the basis of all creation, since Darkness pervades the whole universe. Life cannot be created directly from the Unmanifest God as a No – thing, so a pre-form has to be present that supports the process of manifestation.

Noah can do this with the coding inherent in his name: When the 58 of Noah is reversed to 85 in geomatria it equates with Chen or two forms of grace. Together with the Noah "pre-form" function these energies become a Reshel triangle that supports and establishes creation. Noah as a pre-form then becomes the form that carries primal love and grace as a vital part of the origins of life. His three sons represent the system to do that.

The Selah or divine darkness is contained in Peter/Kaffa, and recalled at Rosslyn by the unadorned altar above the stairs — standing before this altar at the head of the steps, the initiate is tested as to whether he has the grace factor that will allow him to descend into the Ark that Noah has prepared below. The Selah also contains a link in meaning to Moses whom we see clutching the ten commandments on a window niche nearby in the south aisle — *he is depicted with a crescent on his head.* The crescent holds the Selah between its points, and was an early form of Aleph (found in numbers I and I000) and also was personified by Taurus. In fact, Noah lived in the Age of Taurus. This letter Aleph is at the foundation of life, and is so precious it has to be left alone. Aleph is akin to a state of suspension.

The Seven vibration of the Lady Chapel is essentially a female function alluding to a complex energy system, held in natural balance by the Kaffa altar which carries a male seeding aspect. (see Appendix D for fine explanation of the 7 dynamic). The male seed is invisibly small but potent in the human act of procreation, and in sacred geometry the male pole or seed often goes by unnoticed and unadorned. In addition to "hollow stone", Kaf may mean "closed fist". The location of the Kaffa altar in the southeast corner denotes a left brain function, while the letter Yud, in the opposite northwest corner (in the bottom right-hand corner of the roof section carved with stars), carries a right brain function as depicted with an open hand.

The bottom step in the lower chapel carries a Yud seed within a subsystem of the Reshel. The Yud here holds the key to freedom and prosperity found within the Christ Glory pole in the lower chapel. This point then links with the altar above where its male aspect changes to a female aspect. This is a common phenomenon where poles switch roles on higher levels. The Yud seed is said to be connected to the missing capstone on the pyramid, and the apex of the phi rhombus. There are many complex systems at play in the lower chapel but this is not the subject of this book. Suffice it to say that the Kaffa altar on the east wall combines action with the wide step or landing here as part of a process of redemption and cleansing for anyone who is working with the highly advanced light system.

The landing leading down to Lower Chapel
The landing or wide step picks up the codes of many of the subsystems operating in Rosslyn. Buehler sees it as the primary focal point to assimilate all the chapel codes. When fully operative, the central Ulta point on the *Event Horizon* is too powerful for humans to safely interact with its energies when fully operative, so the platform has created a special teleplane (time continuum reality) of its own that can adjust to the individual using it, phasing them into the larger matrix. The Chapel was designed to employ people who were already beyond redemptive requirements, and were "Clear" operators. These then would have been like an inner core of Templars, able to engage with the many systems of light codes held in the chapel/temple.

The wide platform is able to use several systems including all the codes found on the Rose Line which it can unify. Both the Rose Mystica as a seventy-two petalled flower energy system and the Rose Line are used here to do Metatronic redemption work. The idea of redemption is secondary to the basic objective in creative process. Greater numbers can pass through the wide step and burn off dross and be cleansed, as well as enhancing their own soul's work in the area, if needed. It is a good place to go through a redemption process before one descends to the older lower chapel where legend says twelve local families met regularly to discuss esoteric affairs, and refused to leave even when their new castle was erected further down the hill.

The more sensitive you are the more systems you will feel here. One of the systems relates to the Eden tree, as it is here that one can become a worm or bird-serpent (the origins of the Hebrew word Shamir can mean Temple Builder) boring into the centre of the Eden tree (Apprentice Pillar). The wounded archetype has to be healed before the chapel is restored. The wound to the temple (human but also as a literal temple) is open and has to be healed via the wide step. The story of the wounded Apprentice may be untrue but as an energy archetype it is valid. The Path of the Mother goes through the Apprentice pillar where it becomes the Tree of Knowledge associated with the southeast.

We shall now turn our attention to a highly specialised local ley that connects with this wide step. It involves high solar codes. Once assimilated, they are fed into the Mari pillar at the Vau pole and spin in a complex series of rings that pass through the various pillars in the chapel. The Mari pillar and main east window carry a very advanced heliotrope grid that helps expand the earth grids world – wide under the umbrella of what is now known as a Messianic grid. Primary solar codes carried in the heliotrope system latch onto the east wall where the *Event Horizon* tracks the sun, and then the codes are passed to the Mari pillar where it rides this information in a spinner field set in a northwest- southeast axis through the wide step. Spiritual participation is maximised when the sun codes are assimilated as they pass through the wide step. The person standing there is in effect riding the subsystem in a spin field. The Rose Mystica and Eden Tree dynamics project there too to energetically boost, bless and protect the rider.

Chapter Seven: Sun Tracker Ley System and Astronomical Esoterica

Heliotropic Systems

Earth has only one satellite moon today. Once there were two moons however and the female version imploded. Mystics such as Rudolf Steiner also mention a second moon that imploded in our solar system a long time ago, and this moon can be equated with the fallen female pillar in the two pillar system. This had a huge effect on humanity's capabilities to embrace both the male and female aspects of creation There is a sun and moon tracker system (heliotrope) centred on St Mary's south of Rosslyn, which will track the two moons of ancient times within its own rotation, while two separate rider systems that are attached to the basic spinning heliotrope ride each moon and feed back into the main sun spinner. Both moons can be used by a system using non-linear Time. The heliotrope strobes (or "sets") key positions within its spinning field. The twelve divisions or radials are created in each revolution of the spinner. The 12 system is the basic format for all energetic containment fields. For instance, the Layooesh central pillar in the higher Reshel requires a form to connect into, and so either end a twelve pole temple is created to hold the higher field of energy.

A heliotrope is any system that will track the Sun's movements constantly. A heliotrope would amplify any Metatronic system with which it works. According to Buehler, heliotropes can etherically clone themselves many times for temporary spiritual tasks required by the parent system.

"The normal Edinburgh Reshel grid constantly spins, as all the grids do, and will track the Sun as a heliotrope. It can orient in any direction in its spherical field. It can also duplicate itself temporarily to focus on any event of special interest in the Celestial Sphere or in the Planet. It will point itself at the Moon and by aligning with the Sun too it can gather much information in the mental plane. If you imagine the grid as a thought process that is in motion, on a higher plane there needs to be a means for that thought to ground itself in our world. This need only be done with a few key points usually found as cairns or standing stones. The basic grid thus defined physically is a re-entering or re-initialization system containing the grids' essential codes. The alignment may be on stars or on a Critical Rotational Positioning (CRP-see **Appendix F**). A CRP will specially tune a grid based on its alignment within the Earth's geographic consciousness field. The TEMPLA MAR directions are an example of Metatronic CRPs."

There is another specialized heliotrope grid centred on Rosslyn which supports the Edinburgh system, allowing other local places to temporarily lock into the Edinburgh grid so the information is passed into and from the centre at Rosslyn. In the locality a heliotropic penta-star with one elongated arm (see **Figure 18**) was discovered in the El'Ben Loha solar/lunar grid. The pivotal centre of this large spinning field is an ancient site in Roslin Glen. The information thus collected is processed by the Chapel and passed into the Edinburgh grid and the Rose Line (Tavhara).

In Rosslyn Chapel this heliotrope subsystem works through the wide step on the stairway to the crypt. Buehler says of this heliotrope in relation to the wide step:
"The El'Ben Loha axis, that processes the massive amount of Solar and Lunar information, in addition to anything else happening in the stellar realms that affect/resonate with Earths' requirements via the Edinburgh pole and its many links, is recalled on this platform too. Moreover the platform area links in with a ley line we call the Sun Line that goes through the glen and keys into the El'Ben Loha solar/ lunar grid, an advanced heliotrope system of leys in the landscape system that relates also to the Sinclair cup.

When William Buehler was in Scotland, I showed him an ancient sundial placed on the external wall of the fifteenth century Borthwick aisle at Borthwick Church. This was built shortly before Rosslyn and the owners were involved in the Crusades along with the Sinclairs. They were, in fact official Cup Bearers to the St Clairs, which is most significant when you consider the Grail dynamics at play here. Early green men can be seen in the eaves of this church and the sun dial always puzzled me because it was not pointing south. When Buehler extended its alignment he discovered it traversed the glen and arrived at Rosslyn Chapel via a reception point in the Glen. The "Sundial" marked by the stone is not the usual time-keeper in the usual context, it is a moving dial the size of Edinburgh on a cosmic scale.

The reception point in the Glen began to take on special significance. Buehler began to draw a grid with a fifteen pointed star within the basic system that was developing around the Borthwick stone. I have always sensed that a series of ancient picto-glyphs in the adjacent glen held power and significance for the earth and so when the new grid was discovered I gave him a grid reference for them and we saw they were directly placed on the ley between Borthwick, Rosewell and Roslin... I was in the vicinity of these picto-glyphs without realising that Buehler was posing questions on their nature that very day to Thoth/Maia. The landowner showed me a triple spiral his wife had recently uncovered under moss on a mossy sandstone cliff. He also told me of a well that has now silted up, and showed me old maps of its location. When I returned home I read in an e-mail from Buehler that, according to Maia/Thoth, the picto-glyphs keyed into the movements of the Sun and Moon, and also picked up the energies of other local sites, including a sign to the goddess (the triple spiral!) and a well close by! I was delighted that I had been in the right spot at the right time, and such moments are like magic.

The Borthwick pentagram (See **Figure 19**) contains the Reshel system that acts as a Heliotrope constantly tracking the Sun. The information thus collected is processed by the Chapel and passed into the Edinburgh grid and the Rose Line (Tavhara). The grid is very advanced and since its discovery a similar pentagram that keys in a heliotrope system has been identified in southern Norway, stretching from Trondheim to Bergen. I was involved in identifying the one in Norway, and we offer tours there now.

Crichton Miller, author of *The Golden Thread of Time*, had kindly put me in touch with Harald Boehlke regarding his publication *Det Norske Pentagram*, now published in English as *The Viking Serpent*. (When Harald showed me his diagrams I spotted among his many maps the same heliotropic grid that Buehler had produced for the Roslin area, and I asked him to forward it to Buehler for analysis. The Sinclairs were the closest jarls (Norwegian earls) to the Kings of Norway, and it would appear that the grid was set down deliberately, in co-operation with early Irish monks who had been invited to settle there. They marked out astonishing alignments and geometric formations using both human artefacts and natural features such as rocks and caves, as well as cathedrals and monasteries - in the very early centuries (mostly tenth and eleventh)! The grid appears to have been seeded in the very area then controlled by the Sinclairs (then Mores). It seems that as geomancers the Sinclairs not only seeded much of Norway with ley lines but carried this knowledge over the North Sea to Scotland in later centuries. They were the chief jarls in Orkney too, where there is a vast and intricate system of leys that feed into the Tav Hara (Rose) Line discovered by Buehler. Ashley Lambie Cowie has done much to augment the grids there in recent years, with his perception of new and old leys. When this knowledge is freely shared the grids become active since, as thought forms in the mental dimensions, they respond to human acknowledgement. These grids can also be used by Light-Groups using synergic technique. (The Light-Group need not be in the actual physical location of the grids being applied.)

Sirius A, B and C

Within the local landscape Rosslyn and Holyrood appear to ride a sun spinner within the main Reshel, whose centre is at St Mary's Chapel ruins south of Rosslyn. There are always astronomical patterns at play when a temple such as Rosslyn is built, and much of Rosslyn's subtle layout keys in with Orion and Sirius and other star positions. Sirius is a star complex closely connected with the heliotropes discussed earlier. Rosslyn Chapel specializes in human interaction with Nature but is strongly focussed on the Christ energy, a universal transformer of dense energies that keys into the Sirius complex as the new star born from the light processing of Sirius A and B.

Thoth explains that Sirius holds the key for transmutation of galactic karma. The fallen female pillar (equivalent also to the fallen moon) accounts for the main aspect of imbalance in our fallen continuum at both planetary and galactic levels. The fallen stellar components are Alpha Draconis, Omega Draconis and the fallen part of Sirius, while the unfallen (Metatronic/Christic) components are Orion, Pleiades and the unfallen part of Sirius. Astronomers tell of a binary system in Sirius that they call Sirius A and Sirius B. There is a constructive third star Sirius C that acts as an energetic point of balance between the two and is not generally recognised. Interestingly Robert Temple in *The Sirius Mysteries* reveals that the Dogon tribe of Sudan knew of the trilogy of stars in the Sirius complex in ancient times. In ancient Egyptian mythology the figures of God, Isis and Horus contained the Sirius trinity of stars, being ABC respectively. The Golden Child / Christ in Rosslyn is like the Grail that has to be discovered.

Within the Middle East in the Al Bar Akhim grid (centred on Qumran) Jerusalem is A, Mecca is B and Al Wadjh is C. (An expansion of that grid includes Istanbul, Mecca and Jerusalem as and strata strike a harmonic in the center of the soul's Atoma or 'inner heart sun', which is the composite of all seven chakras.

points A, B and C respectively. Jerusalem rides the Sun Line in a heliotrope centred on St Catherine's on Mount Sinai. This information is carried back west to Ireland via the path of the Mother.)

In Scotland the start of the important ley from the Iona/Staffa couplet to Lindisfarne passes through the Holyrood Park area in Edinburgh and uses three points that act as a trinity representing the Sirius Star dynamics. Iona is seen as Sirius A, Staffa as star B and Duart Castle on the Isle of Mull as star C. This dynamic can be duplicated in human designed temples, often not known of by the builders but nevertheless fitting a pattern of higher design.

The centres of such temples as Rosslyn seem to be spinners for heliotropes, with a rider system set off-centre for more effective access. In Chartres the equivalent is the Labyrinth as centre with the Bishop's throne/chair as the rider system.
In Rosslyn Chapel, the Kaffa/Peter altar represents Sirius A; the wide step/landing on the stairs represents Sirius B and the Eden Tree (Apprentice Pillar) Sirius C. The Eden Tree, with serpents at its base, makes possible the inversion of the Trapped Light into the Full Light. In the process the light available to us has been redeemed and freed of its bondage within matter.

Within the landscape surrounding Rosslyn, the threefold system that Sirius represents is echoed by the Sun Dog effect described below. This effect is caused by a light shining through the east wall at sunrise on St Matthew's Day. Awareness of this phenomenon drew attention to its correlation with the Sun Line (ley) line that runs through Roslin Glen, which will be discussed below.

The Red Star that amplifies the Mazuriel alignment in chapel
John Ritchie in *Rosslyn Revealed: A Library in Stone*, O Books 2006

writes of an aperture in the large east window (clerestory level) that is pentagonal in shape. On St Matthew's Feast Day (Autumn equinox) the chapel is so aligned that the rising sun shines through this aperture and sends a red beam of light onto the back west wall. The west wall was always left blank until the Victorians added an organ gallery and opened it up for music to flood the chapel. Just as many prehistoric monuments are aligned with equinoxal sunrises, the chapel honours the skies in an identical arrangement. One site in Ireland that is little known but provides a very good example of this in the Lough Crew set of cairns in County Meath. Ritchie's discovery of the red pentagonal light box fits closely with recent research done by Buehler on the Sirius complex in the chapel. Buehler calls Ritchie's discovery the Penta Star. Often new discoveries add more physical layers to what Buehler has determined to exist in the etheric layer of the chapel.

Applying spiritual dynamics in this phenomenon, the red penta-star can be correlated with the Sun shining through a region of ice crystals above the Earth causing refraction. A double sun-image phenomenon ("Sun-Dogs" or "Dragons' Eyes") provides the "parahelia" effect noted below. This dynamic can be correlated with the penta-star representing the Sun. It would be used in combination with the red light to create a triple image of the sun reflected on the west wall of the chapel. The parallel spiritual process can be likened to what occurs when sunlight is refracted by ice crystals in high cloud formations causing what is scientifically called the Parhelia Effect. The earth used to have an intact spherical Ice Canopy around it in earlier times, and the images seen as duplicate Suns bracketing the sun are commonly called "Sun Dogs" these days. Buehler says:

"A Sun Dog is a separate image of the Sun but at both sides of the Sun caused by ice crystals. So you have the real sun but an image on each side of it. The triple layered Sun links in with Mazuriel the manifest Sacred Heart that lies at the centre of all Central Suns. The one sun becomes threefold representative of how the light works in three Time continua of past, presnt and future simultaneously."

Within the Reshel systems of the chapel, if working with the red penta star the light operators in the chapel would work routinely at ground level with one teleplane to key in with the geometry of the pillars etc, **Figure 20** shows the Reshel system centred on the Rose Line within the chapel. The Ulta or Zayin point lies on the Rose Line where both halves of the Reshel meet. The first teleplane lies along the east wall and is the Event Horizon on the Rose line, which the ancients call "Tavhara".

There is also a simultaneous light process via the Mari Pillar, joining the Rose Line system to a higher Christic system that begins geometrically at the level of the niches where the apostles once were placed. Buehler calls this level the Apostolic plane. It works as follows: When the Zayin point that shares both halves is dragged down into the Mari pillar position, it then aligns with the Ulta pole, activating a new higher level known as the Christic system. The triple suns are now placed above and level with the Mari pillar. **Figure 21** shows the Reshel system centred on the Mari pillar and using a new teleplane at the Apostolic level/plane within a 3:1 rectangle based on Solomon's Temple. The 3:1 rectangle forms a reality plane in which there is a double pentagon that seeds the spiritual centre, and it is appropriate to use this with the Parhelia and Red Star phenomena. The central Mari pillar marks the "Holy Point" (the new Shiyn pole) where a person can stand, image a Parhelia to activate it, and also link into the floor level. A red penta-light shines through on the Equinoxes when the chapel is aligned with the rising sun. The Reshel stars either side of the Mari pillar represent the Sun Dogs on each side of the central pentalight, assuming it is used as a Parhelia. See **Figure 21**. There is also a type of alchemical union of opposites here as Virgo is in alignment during St Matthew's Feast Day, and this becomes a "mystic marriage" between the virgin and the seed/staff. This is supported as

Mari Pillar with its Stem and Blossom (budding staff) glyph correspondence.

When operating this system the initiate extends his/her personal pillar vertically up to the Apostolic plane to be at a height to view the Parhelia effect (physically or etherically), using the red light as the centre. When operating the Reshel at this higher Apostolic level one accesses the etheric chamber within the Pyramid called the Kh-an-at that relates to the old star Betelgeuse, which plays a complementary role to Rigel. The lower Reshel plane contains Rigel in that spot, with which the initiate could link by intention. The purpose of being on the Apostolic level is to merge with those codes. The two poles of the refracted light become important in defining the nature of the Creation Field above the Mari Pillar. The new "Earth star" that Earth will become in the Great Shift lies within the Blue Star complex of Rigel in Orion, and Betelgeuse will there be seen as our red star partner.

This is a particular example of how the Reshel moves to accommodate specific spiritual purposes and reflects the intent in the geometry. In effect, the operator is raising the Shamir/ Serpent on the Staff as in John 3: 13-14.
"And no man hath ascended up to heaven, but he that came down from heaven, even the Son of man which is in heaven.
And as Moses lifted up the serpent in the wilderness, even so must the Son of man be lifted up that whosoever believes in Him should not perish but have everlasting life."

(The Serpent Staff relates to life generation as well as the physical healing of the Tribes and other groups.)

Thoth has confirmed the Parhelia becomes a Dione Couplet after the viewer has been cleansed and aligned. The left star position marks the pole for the past Metatronic Sun, the right star the pole for the future Metatronic Sun and the central Mari pillar position represents our present Sun in the Oritronic realm which is being transformed and made a part of the new Universe.

The Sun to the left generates new forms while the Sun to the right represents the place of dominion. The best (Metatronic) wisdom of the past is the basis for our own present valid wisdom that makes the future. Although the future is already formed it is dynamic, always changing as the Cycles continue to produce change. "Dominion" is used in the sense it represents its own Creation process administered in all three modes by the Solarians, etc, in the distant Capricornian future. This polarization of the central Sun can form other valuable systems, for example the 'Dione Couplet' procedure. In light work it is not necessary to wait for the Sun to cooperate with a Parhelia action, as it can be etherically created any time required. See **Figure 22**.

Linking in the theme of the Apostolic plane, the Apostles were a synergic light group with the standard twelve functions that apply within light work. The thirteenth, Christos' input comes via the Parhelia dynamic. The dynamic of the thirteenth is further explained in Chapter 9. The earlier spelling of Rosslyn was Roslinne which according to Buehler can be translated from the Scottish Gaelic and interpreted as "Brood hen, brood of twelve or line of twelve" referring to the Apostles or other groups of twelve, and the thirteenth sign could be seen as the cockerel that seeds the line of twelve brood hens. Interestingly the traditional symbol for the St Clairs is the cockerel in the clan's Arms, who traditionally faces the sunrise, and is driven by the wind to rotate and spin. The analogy seems to offer another form of link between sun and earth and the spinner field as well as attuning to the creation field by changing geographic orientation.

Of course the initiate does not have to physically operate the apostolic plane system on St Matthew's Day, for he works in non-linear time always. The chapel design is set with a variety of ground matrices, and this is but one of the latest to be discovered. On the Autumn equinox the effects would be more pronounced.

Parhelia Axes from Chapel

If there is a parhelic effect, the Sun Dogs will normally appear about twenty two degrees either side of the sun. The triple sun seen through the window at Rosslyn reflects the central axis on the main east direction and the two other ley lines going through Borthwick and Newbattle, each offset at 22 degrees. This is most significant as the so-called Sun Line that runs through the ancient sandstone glyphs in Roslin Glen to Borthwick Chapel is twenty one or two degrees offset from true east, at about 111°T (T= True North), and when a complimentary line is drawn at 68°T to reflect the other Sun Dog at 21/22 degrees, this line links many sites that are related to the Sun, such as Newbattle Abbey whose Kerr sun heraldry became the symbol for the Lothians., and Winton House then owned by the Seton family. This second offset line is the Grace factor according to Thoth/Maia and connects with the etheric position of Sirius C etc. It is interesting that the names of two farms further out on the line are named Jerusalem and Samuelstone, which suggest two poles reflecting Grace/Power and Light Codes respectively. There would be a third central pole representing Love. See **Figure 23**.

The stellar charts ascribed by Rab Wilkie esoteric astronomer for Rosslyn at the vernal equinoctial position in 2008 indicate that, due to its true east orientation, the chapel will align with Orion and various Grail archetype constellations in the sky at the cardinal (four main) directions. Moreover the 111 degree alignment that follows the Sun Line ley through the glen is very interesting, and shows the whole of the Grail constellation will have risen as the Sun aligns with the 111° T. This line leads to the residence of the Borthwicks who were the official cup-bearers to the Sinclairs, with their legendary engrailed cup!

When Mercury rises a little later in the day Spica is found in the centre of a rare configuration formed by a triangle of Venus, Mars and Mercury. Can this be why the god Mercury is carved overlooking the lower chapel, gazing upon the Sun Line in the glen?

Rigel our mother planet star in Orion rises in the 111° direction while Saturn the ruler of Aquarius aligns with Denebelo in Leo. (While Rigel is a star in our universe, in the Metatronic universes the planets are contained within the parent star, not in a ballistic orbit due to the low frequency of this Continuum. They effectively become a unified body with the Star. The Earth is likewise becoming a New Earth star, rather than a planet and the present Sun will be left in its own orbit. We are used to thinking of stars as hydrogen explosions, not as sentient beings with many light bodies, as also are the Planets. They have coexistent light bodies including a physical range but in a form of parallel reality. Highly evolved humans similarity can contain a human soul formed by five or more souls in a synergically unified single soul, where one soul is the "body soul.")

Due to William Buehler recognizing this local heliotrope a few years ago, the astronomical charts were examined, and revealed a highly significant alignment, which brings in all the major players in the skies for our own quantum shift in consciousness. For full details of the chart by Rab Wilkie (rab@peterboro.net) see **APPENDIX E**

Chapter Eight : Some Stellar Alignments

Thoth says that there is an unfallen star "Sekhet" in the scabbard of Orion, of which Rosslyn holds the earthly equivalent position. The star is unfallen because although some of the universe shifted its stellar layout upon the Fall, Sekhet never fell from grace and remains undisturbed in the Unfallen or Metatronic energy system. This star is located just under Alnilam in the Belt of Orion.

A major grid in Europe is the ASTARA equilateral triangle, functioning as a Flower of Life, in which Rosslyn is the apex correlating with Sekhet in the same triangle in Orion. (Saiph relates to Rome and Rigel to Sintra in Portugal.) This would explain why the area around Rosslyn has been used for many aeons for worship according to Maia/Thoth.

Esotericists knew of two orbits of Venus that link in with Earth's orbit. The 225 day orbit and the 260 day orbit represent the Oritronic and Metatronic orbits respectively, much in the same way that the Mayan culture portrayed Venus with two similar length orbits. One important NASA scientist who toured with me for some days told me that he too had realized that the Templar and the Mayan cultures had come up with these two exact orbits for Venus, but he could not reconcile this inner knowledge with his scientific training that demanded "proof". His discoveries in Moon research are well known, but his forays into the unknown world of the Mayans remain his private hobby....Leonardo Da Vinci without doubt knew of the two Venus Orbits, and Buehler has made fascinating links between Da Vinci's graphics and the European Reshel grids. For instance, when you place Da Vinci's Vitruvian man over Western Europe the pair of Venusian orbits are indicated, with Rome, Sintra and Rosslyn in key nodes of what Buehler calls the Titan Oceanus grid. The high chakra over the man's crown chakra becomes the Holy Isle of Ruta, the Atlantean isle that sank after the priests there transferred all their knowledge into Europe, Egypt and other areas including the ancient site near Callanish on Lewis in the Outer Hebrides. (As with many of these prehistoric sites we see only the last stages of development intact today, the bogs having claimed many of the earlier monuments.) See **Figure 24**.

It is very possible that there were early Masons who understood these Reshel dynamics in which truly the As Above So Below took place here on Earth. Lord Burlington's Chiswick House in London is an excellent example. I have successfully dowsed the geometric nodes in his home in Chiswick where the layout of ancient paths in the grounds key directly into the Metatronic alignments, where in our fallen universe the Denebola star in the Leo constellation is the equivalent position for Mazuriel, the central Sun of all suns in our wider *Attasic* Universe (a universe shared by all universes at the highest level of reality).

Chapter Nine: The Lower Chapel

Templar Bosses

The two miniature temples on the bosses overlooking the stairs leading to the lower Chapel are larger than usual. Each displays very interesting undersides of two church windows with central pillars, while the windows in the left temple are more elongated and there is a Templar Cross above its wider central pillar.

There are Templar symbols throughout the chapel but their cross is rarely seen except in the lower chapel since that chapel was built earlier, more than likely at a time when they were legitimate in Scotland. As discussed earlier the lower chapel contains the Christic half of the Basic Reshel, the *Shekinah* half being in the upper chapel. The Resh point of the Christic half is in a small room offset to the northeast of the lower chapel, in the small sacristy to the left – this point is reached via a nesting of "L"s so that there are several time gates being operated, as illustrated in Fig 8 earlier. The stacked L pattern also exists in St Piat's Chapel at Chartres, another of the cathedrals which incorporates knowledge of the Reshel.

The Alpha Pole

When we are in the Lower Chapel at Rosslyn we key into European grids such as the Astara and Titan Oceanus, for a new Christic station was opened within the L system in 1998 as the grounding of the Schiehallion Planetary Christic ALPHA pole. Schiehallion is a mountain in Perthshire that towers above the magical Glen Lyon, a glen that is in direct harmonics with Rosslyn via an angle known as the Bethlehem or "Nuur" angle. The angle derives its name from the angle formed between the latitude of the Giza Plateau and Bethlehem, which is 26°18′ From the Rose Line at St Mary's (centre of Roslin area matrix) a line runs at this angle to the northwest and passes through Fortingall, which lies below Scotland's high fairy mountain of

Schiehallion. Fortingall in Glen Lyon is an ancient seat of worship in Perthshire. The mountain and Glen Lyon/Fortingall are related energetically, in much the same way as Edinburgh's Arthur's Seat relates to Roslin Glen and Rosslyn Chapel. (Esoteric tradition has it that Fortingall was, and still is, the location of the "Academy of Christ" in which the Messiah was trained prior to the Advent.) As a land mass they form mountain and glen couplets with the masculine pole . See **Figure 25**

The Judas Stone

My identification of the Judas stone at the Resh point was no accident. This was a damaged relic brought in at the time the chapel underwent essential repair work on the foundations of the retaining wall, and the shelving was erected to house such fragments discovered when restoring the foundations. (I feel the Judas stone may have lain in the alcove in the outer right hand wall above the stairs to the lower chapel. The broken stone ribbing is still plain to see where a statue was torn away. This alcove was level with the Kaffa altar above the stair landing.)

This link with Judas was very appropriate because he carries two levels within his Yud/Yuda dynamic: the Yuda Ishcarioth and Yuda Not-Ishcarioth (John 14:22). The placement of his coding at the Christos point in the chapel is significant. As with many of the discoveries made in connection with the Reshel, I felt this stone spoke to me. William Buehler was able to explain its wider significance. He told me that the Olgive Christic mysteries were shared in the garden of Gethsemane, and those who built the chapel understood these mysteries. Yuda in his Ishcariot form bore a fire soul in the lower temporal plane, and is connected to foundational fire (this is found in the Esh-Karioth" translation and the function of the Esh/Esha souls in Genesis). Like Prometheus who is one of many fire signs in the chapel, Yuda sacrifices himself so that he can renew himself (this time in his Not-Ishcariot form). Yuda Ishcariot is so holy and full of grace he is set apart and has to be willing to fall in order that the group of twelve can grow synergically. When he emerges anew he becomes the thirteenth disciple beyond the normal twelve, and this is highly pertinent to our times. The glen has become more active and is perceived by many to be the real powerhouse of energy, the chapel being a decoy to some real extent, as its carvings are a mere reflection of the more active etheric processes that are ongoing. Due to the increase in energy in the glen the Yuda or Yud codes were successfully inserted. Judas' thirty pieces of silver carry the Lammed/30 code, which is drawn as a golden ratio spiral. This spiral is so common to organic life forms, so being inserted at this point of time in a chapel dedicated to the processes of regeneration suggests that the chapel has come into its own time regarding its purpose. Buehler perceives that the disciple that Yeshua loved in the Gospel of John was indeed Judas. At a higher level Judas becomes the Judas Not Ishcariot form related to the No-Thing in the Selah dynamic. In ancient Hebrew of the Jewish Scriptures, when something or someone is described as a Not or No-Thing or Not Somebody, since the word is really part of a language of light codes, it is actually describing something of a higher function that can be equated with the divine indwelling self and the basic Foundation of all actions as the divine source of Life. The coding in the letter sets up a pre-form to the actual manifestation. Early holy languages held words for That Which is Not, as a necessary stage of the process before things manifest.

In John 13:23-31, Yeshua appears to have sacrificed Yuda in the Ishcariott form to Satan. In his higher form though, as Not Ishcariot, Judas is held safe during the present Fall continuum. Buehler's interpretation suggests that Judas would have understood that he had to deliver his Master but that his action bore no detriment to his soul, as he was protected on a higher level. It is interesting to note that I recognised the Judas stone around the time that the recently discovered Gospel of Judas was written about in *National Geographic*, in which Judas is shown to have agreed to betray Yeshua personally, so that he endures the karmic repercussions that such an action entails. By translating the Greek gospel of John back into Hebrew many clues were found as to the sacred mystery writings it contains. John the disciple as a pure love vibration would have fulfilled the Yud dynamic, while Judas is the pure light form that is the thirteenth disciple. When twelve poles generate a thirteenth thus, the old twelve all transit to a new level where they remain as a twelve synergic vibration until the next shift in consciousness is upon us. In other words, the Not Ishcariot transmutes fire into our continuum so that the whole group of twelve will be transformed and empowered. Each of the twelve represents a specialised strand of DNA, for the Metatonic human has twelve strands of DNA activated at molecular level. Assisting in designing a new version of the normal twelve-strand DNA model has become a passionate project for Buehler over recent years. Within the Zodiac the thirteenth sign is seen as the unicorn in the future, or the dolphin at present: Delphinus in Capricorn. Hence perhaps the popularity of these symbols today, as they speak to the collective higher self.

Chapter Ten: Interpreting and Expanding on the Reshel

Truth

For some who reflect on the nature of truth it seems dynamic, shifting in scope and degree. As one matures there are new levels of truth, for awareness is dependent on the level of understanding each of us possesses. For many who visit Rosslyn Chapel, that is how the game of truth is played; every visit reveals a new light on matters. I personally know of those who declare "truths" about the chapel which they later revoke. Their theories that were once so precious retreat in later years as the soul matures, and the ego retreats. From a human perspective then, within truth there is always movement, as truth in all realms engages in its own changing pattern of light. Each moment it presents us with a new facet or jewel, still subject to the universal law of change.

Yet the concept of truth belongs to the moment and beyond the moment simultaneously; within our linear world a relative state of truth presides, and yet within this human Oritronic/half light state man can contemplate a divine state or supreme Being, where truth does not alter. When we talk of an absolute or ultimate truth, we are imagining a state where the deepest levels of reality are accessed and embraced with love and purity. That unchanging centre is best expressed as the void (the Suspension Point or Selah in Hebrew) out of which everything becomes known and presented. An absolute truth can only exist beyond time and space, in what in this book has been called the Metatronic realm with its much higher range of frequencies. Since, through its intricate design, the chapel provides a bridge to this higher world, we can sense a greater truth or a greater whole when we enter the chapel. It is not just the plethora of symbols and exquisite craftsmanship displayed in the carvings that inspires; there is something beyond. Even if we cannot articulate it or make it tangible, we know that the mystery of the divine is somehow there. Many past visitors have quietly wept when they complete a tour with me, as they begin to see how deep the coding is in the chapel, and one engineer described it as an expression in stone of all the spiritual mysteries available to man. Indeed only those who were armed with inner knowledge borne of direct experience could have created such an edifice.

Reshel Dynamics at Play

For me, the spiritual system of the Reshel contains a dynamic growing pattern of divine light codes that mirrors many facets and levels of humanity. According to Buehler, the Reshel is a spiritual light system that manages, creates and adjusts to spiritual events in a safe manner, linking Matter and Anti-Matter or the Oritronic and Metatronic. It is not a religion or a dogma but an interface tool for arranging life patterns in a way we can use them for the highest good and in an increasingly Metatronic context in step with the evolution of Gaia and the Race of Man.

It may be helpful here to present an example from my own life to show how this works.

About five years ago I was leading a small tour of the Cairnpapple henge area in West Lothian, and we entered the old cemetery that surrounds the ancient preceptory of the Knights of St John. There was a grave slab facing us that had a carving on it that looked uncannily like a Jewish menorah. As my female companion and I were staring at it in silence, it suddenly became alive as if the object came out of the stone toward us and had a life of its own. We discovered a few minutes later that both of us had felt this energy from the gravestone, and something had touched us deeply. That evening when I returned home and opened up my e-mails, I read of news from Jordan, which described a new grid a geomancer had found in the Middle East, and he named it the Menorah Grid, a three-fold Reshel system! I decided to visit the region where the grid lay (in Jordan) as I felt spiritually drawn to do so.

When I reached Amman I had arranged to visit the geomancer, and he invited me to travel across the desert with friends who were Bedouins, following the ancient routes. I found that these nomads were sensitive to the earth energies and other spiritual phenomena, and every night they lit incense of the Syrian rue in my tent to aid my dreams. I was asked to relate my dreams to them in the morning as this was one way of "reading the land and its messages". However, immediately the powerful vapour rose through the air each night I saw visions, and wrote to Buehler about them. He replied that I had seen many esoteric Templar symbols – including ancient Hebrew number codes for a series of grace factors, and what is called the teleplane (forms a continuum reality in Time). On the third night I saw John the Baptist in a definitive posture and wearing scarlet and gold, which apparently were the colours traditionally associated with him. This reading of the land by recognising key codes connected to the spiritual function and destiny of the land is one way in which the leys in the area are activated. It is not with intent to manipulate the leys, but with grace and innocence that we can be effective. I certainly did not plan any of the series of events that unfurled during my journey in the desert, and yet I felt entrusted by the nomads for a particular mission that, within the unfolding leys of the Reshel, impacted on a wider spiritual mission. When we dedicate ourselves to knowing the higher truth, and being of service for the good of all then we have to trust the higher beings to lead us on in such a journey.

In this particular journey I had linked into the consciousness of a very recently discovered grid that was named the Ali Araat grid. An experienced Reshel light group led by Buehler in Colorado had been working to "activate" it one week prior to the 9-11 events and another group scheduled the grid's next level of activation on the date of 9-11. I had traveled out there a few months after that tragedy, an event that marked a planetary shift in consciousness and caused initially a huge humanitarian swell of compassion.

The Ali-Araat grid became a vital Mideast grid seeding the whole European Reshel systems in the creation of the Planetary MESSIANIC grid on 9-11. The creation of this grid was effected by massive changes including volcanic activity of the new island (seamount) in Hawaii which boosted the Hawaiian "Roil" pole function through a kundalini surge (explanation of the Roil pole follows). This action in Hawaii had direct input from the European and Mideast Reshel matrices. The huge surge of love and empathy in the Racial Mind/Soul (collective) was "organized" by the newly activated Metatronic planetary matrix.

At this point it may be helpful to introduce the notion of the Earth/Gaia as a sentient being, and to look at the roles of the Middle East and Europe. First we might picture the planet as a large brain with all its connecting ley lines acting as though they were nerve pathways in the brain. The unified Gaia and Racial Mind/Soul are combined as a left and right brain.

Gaia as Consciousness
Independent of specialised light workers, the planet is sentient and responds to our collective thoughts – the Reshel also responds to us as a specialized matrix within the Racial mind, and its nerve pathways are patterns that are divine thought forms placed as ley lines across the earth. The Reshel patterns are part of a higher response to the call of Gaia to return home. Put another way, the Reshel is light in patterns that assist consciousness on all levels and in all realms and across time. Gaia consciousness not only pertains to the human race – it is heavily interwoven with Earth as a planet, the Sun, the Moon and the planets of the solar system, and other stellar areas in the Celestial sphere.

We can consider Europe to be the right forebrain of the Planet and the Racial Mind. In our more familiar level of application it is the female pole with the essential vibration of 7 (Sheeba). (See **Appendix D** for an analysis by Aine Armour- Barrett of the 7 vibration in vital connection with the 8 vibration in readiness for the current phase of transition.) The composite Reshel grid system in Europe is called the "Bar-Sheeba", or "Son of the Sheeba", a goddess dedication that the Templars followed closely. By comparison the Middle East is the left forebrain of the planet and is essentially a male pole inseminating the other forebrain with fire-codes conditioned by the various religions of that area's Racial Mind/Soul in the Metatronic harmonics beyond fallen ideologies.

In the human brain there is a synaptic gap between the right and left lobes - Rev Maia has channeled intricate information that may help explain the significance of this Selah bridge in our brains that is echoed at a planetary level. She writes of the gap being linked to a critical rotational pulse (CRP) in the brain. This dynamic is critical to understanding grids, orientation, and rotation. See **Appendix G** for details.

Both forebrains have been connected by the ICARUS ley from Sligo Bay to Mount. Sinai and Mount Katherine for the last fourteen to fifteen thousand years. Two mountains are often found at each end of a major ley line, as in the case of this grid. In Ireland Ben Bulben and Queen Maeve's tomb become dipoles with the sea between them. In the Reshel this is akin to the splitting of the stone or land mass that occurs in the Chief Corner Stone or Resh point. Creation depends upon a basic duality – in the past the one *had* to become two in order for anything to be activated. Many right brain Reshel grids in Europe have been rediscovered over the last 500 years or so and even more so in the last 30 years, but until recently only the Ali Araat grid in the left forebrain served to complement them.
This one grid served a male seeding role. It can be viewed at
  www.shameer-orion.org/pdf/GrdAliAraat03.pdf.

There is a cautionary tale to tell here too. There is always a lower and a higher expression of the self according to how much courage there is to face one's potential, and this holds true at a planetary level also. The true essence or spiritual function of the Middle East as the left (male) forebrain is to order its thinking (as they did in their Golden Age of Science long before any Renaissance in the west). However, in our Oritronic world the higher essence is not expressed, and its polarity rises to the surface. In this instance the Middle East tends to become bogged down in the lower (female) expression of itself, manifesting in chaotic systems and a tendency to continually fragment. Meanwhile Europe as the right (female) forebrain in its true essence would blossom as a highly creative and expressive culture if not held down by dogma and bureaucracy. Europe, however, often gets bogged down in details that do not further its cause or express its essence - its own lower frequencies are more male instead .

Change is apparent. Recent history shows there have been efforts for humanity to shift – for small countries within Europe to rule far more autonomously, and for new, more centralized structures to form in the Middle East, and so on. There is inevitable confusion when old systems attempt to shift, and above all fear of change has to be dispelled at core level. The more the void can be trusted, the more creative a response will arise. Indeed, in the third millennium there is a growing acceptance in the global mind/ soul to process Metatronic light codes.

Returning to the valid image of the Earth as a large brain that is both affecting and affected by our own conscious thoughts, there is a point that accesses Gaia and processes all her resonant racial / global mind and all incumbent systems. This is called the Roil/ Royale point and can be found at the back of the head. Within the Earth, it is situated at Hawaii.
Greece is at the ajna/brow point that connects the two forebrains, and sends the information to Hawaii where it is

upgraded so to speak. The composite grids of Europe have been extended into North America, an initiative partly seeded during the 1398 expedition funded by the first Prince of Orkney Henry Sinclair.

These Reshel grids exist to organize Metatronic, including the Christic consciousness and the formats that support it in the etheric Earth itself, as well as in the wider universe. It is nevertheless up to those who dwell on the Earth to choose to evolve in consciousness and tune into these earth grids as a genuine impulse that is available in the ether now. While certain sites on earth mark nodes in the geometry, and certain points in chapels and temples mark similarly on a microcosmic scale, the system of light is so fluid these points only act as a base template from which the earth or the chapel adjust their etheric movements according to what is spiritually required, so any attachment to one particular spot by a light worker would be unwise. It is true that every few thousand years there is a "New Age", but, as Buehler points out, our time now is about a totally new time continuum being generated that has always been there in real time, but only coming into a state of being for us as we shed the layers of illusion. Perhaps the challenge is for each of us to welcome this new paradigm and find our unique ways of engaging with it.

Postscript: The Reshel Is a Spiritual Technology:

A Brief Introduction

prepared by William Buehler and Carol Mann

1. What is a Spiritual Technology?

It is an intentional collaboration of the combined consciousness of humans, angels and nature's elemental beings which can be focused toward a higher spiritual purpose. Under the guidance of Higher States of Being, and using certain prescribed sacred formats, those focused collective thought forms of light act as a consciousness bridge between heaven and earth. The bridge can be utilized to download spiritually governed upgrades for the earth and all its inhabitants.

2. What specifically is the RESHEL as a spiritual technology and what does it do?

The word Reshel comes from Hebrew and can be translated as "chief headstone of God". The Reshel is a specific geometric format which facilitates linking into the full light spectrum energies of our evolutionary future. These energies are called the Metatron, named for the highest Archangel Metatron, whose state of being is the full light spectrum.

The earth is currently in the fallen, half-light spectrum in which both light and dark energies are present. With the assistance of Higher Programs of Light and the participation of our own consciousness, the earth is reclaiming her original path in the full light spectrum. The Reshel format offers access to the energies of our Metatronic future and allows those energies to infuse into the present. The total exchange serves to catalyze the ascension of the earth to the full light spectrum.

More specifically; the Reshel format activates sacred geometric relationships which function simultaneously in the realms of consciousness, energy and form. The Reshel establishes a containment field resonant with the Sacred Heart of God and Divine Grace, allowing accurate inter-dimensional communication and elegant meshing of fallen and Metatronic dynamics.

3. What are the historical origins of the Reshel?

The technology is part of an extensive Program of Light. It is to be used through twenty evolutionary cycles, as an integral part of Earth's eventual return to the full light spectrum. The Reshel is overseen by the Seraphic ENNEAD (Group of Nine). Under the ENNEAD, the Reshel is then assigned to the Michael Mandate. The "download" in each cycle would of course be calibrated by the Higher Agencies to be no more and no less than appropriate given the dynamic, ever-changing nature of how all things unfold toward a reconnection to the full light spectrum. Right now we are in the last part of the 19th cycle. This cycle began during the phase leading to the final sinking of Atlantis, approximately 9500 BCE. So, according to our best understanding, the Reshel system would date back about half a million years.

Programs of Light are encoded into the living matrices of all creation...which here include the earth's energies as expressed in ley lines and topographical features, our DNA and the DNA of all living things at all levels of sentience. And these evolutionary programs are operating whether or not we are awake and consciously participating.

Throughout history there have been groups of souls who have accessed higher consciousness and realities on the inner planes, where the presence of sacred formats and how they operate is revealed. The knowledge gained of spiritual technologies could be used and amplified on purpose. Significant ancient Temple sites, architecture, art, sites used for ritual purposes and earth grid locations have been intentionally chosen, designed and maintained to amplify the Reshel format.

We also know from the Akashic records of our own souls, that individuals with the sacred knowledge gathered in what today we call "Light Groups" to participate in the conscious exchanges of sacred light codes. Until now the awareness and knowledge of how these spiritual technologies work have been kept secret in order to preserve the knowledge intact. In the old, fear-based paradigm, sacred meta-scientific knowledge of the true workings of the universe was a threat to those in politics and religion whose level of consciousness was limited to power over others rather than true spiritual sovereignty and empowerment. Those who were aware of such meta-scientific knowledge could be punished by death.

4. How was the Reshel used by the Templars?

The evidence of knowledge of the Reshel is found as patterns, geometric relationships and grid lines intentionally incorporated by the Templars in their buildings, zymology and ritual. Since all of this was secret, nothing overt would have been written. However the chosen locations, interconnections, architectural proportions and even the patterns of travel and trade routes used by the Templars reflect the Reshel geometries. The Reshel was one important way the Templars exercised their commitment to move forward the Ascension dynamics in the planetary and collective racial mind/soul of the earth.

5. What was/is Rosslyn's historical significance in relation to the Reshel?

We are told by Maia/Thoth that this has been a Temple site at least three other times since the Atlantean period. Rosslyn

Chapel and its Glen continue to keep alive the action of these ancient time lines .It is the "Resh", the consciousness pole of the "chief headstone of God" in the Edinburgh Grid. As such, Rosslyn synthesizes all the actions in the extensive Edinburgh Grid (which includes the Grail dynamics), and upgrades them into Metatronic formats. Since the 1400's, Rosslyn's living earth temple location, its sacred architecture, and the participation of initiates in the Reshel, have played a key part in shaping Ascension programming for nations in Europe and in the Americas.

6. What is the importance of Rosslyn in the current activation of Reshel Ascension dynamics?

As part of the acceleration of our times, Rosslyn and the Glen have been upgraded and reconnected in new, expanded ways to the devic, angelic, solar, lunar and stellar realms. This has created a resonant harmonic with other grids around the planet which are also rapidly expanding and upgrading their Ascension capacities.

7.What can happen if I visit Rosslyn Chapel?

Just by standing in the energy field of Rosslyn for about a half hour, all of its visitors are being offered a subtle upgrade in consciousness.

Copyright (c) 2006, by Carol Mann and William Buehler

ALOII LANGUAGE: The most ancient of languages was the "Aloii," which was derived from the electrical waves in the brain, that when firing, create actual "fire letters." This is true for the electrical impulses in the heart-brain (the neurons within the heart) as well. It is a sacred Lemurian/Atlantean/Dannan language created from the hard-soft dodeca-faces of Mudic spin found in the Dione Couplet dynamic.

"The DIONE Process taps into the Mudic harmonics, which consist of the Od and the Attim. The Od is the soft face of -the Earth's dodecahedral matrix while the Attim is the hard face. As these frequencies spin in their couplet spirals they charge in either hard or soft mode, depending on the degree of tilt and velocity of spin. It is from these Mudic harmonics that the Sacred languages are registered. The Od harmonic is that which carries the most powerful Matter to Spirit magnetic clearing capability. The DIONE Process taps into the Mudic harmonics it brings the Od and Attim patterns or codes into the physical/ etheric bodies aligning them to the natural dodecahedral spin of the crystalline lattices of the DNA which in turn, resonate to the natural dodecahedral spin of the planet. This resonation creates a synergistic Oneness that eliminates the magnetic polarity. The many components of the DIONE healing create a unique format for release of lower magnetic, karmic programming within the holistic system." (Excerpt from the Dione Couplet information in www.spiritmythos.org)

ATTASIC UNIVERSE:: A Universe reality that includes all Universes. From "Akashic Definitions" (www.spiritmythos.org): "A neutral universal field that holds the balance between the universe and anti-universe preventing these two potentials from coming into direct contact with each other, which would result in the destruction of both. It is the unified field of all consciousness where there is no separation. All time fields and universal

The Attasic Universe is the charge of release from time / space / matter divisions."

EVENT HORIZON: The point of passage between space-time continua where **awareness** of new potentials is so expansive as to **induce** the passage. In Reshel application the core dynamic of the Event Horizon is the coded continuum-plane that generates its own apparent reality in 3-dimensional Time and Space. Each half of the Reshel has its Event Horizon that is coded by the central Neutra Universe teleplane. The Neutra teleplane has two planes that match with the two Event Horizons when the Reshel halves are base-to-base. (The Neutra Universe is the usually invisible space between the two base Event Horizons.) As the two Reshel halves go through their cyclic interaction they each carry their Event Horizons with them thus maintaining continuity through the cycle and refreshing when in contact with the Neutra teleplane.

EYE OF RA: The Eye of Ra is a Breast Plate of Metatron, and be correlated with a Universal Star Gate. The golden ratio rhombus is its best geometric design as a practical working system; it also uses the complementary Reshel or "Techad" (ISIS Eye), another Breast Plate, to organize many systems in correct sequence of creation and dis-creation in the Flashing Universe dynamic cycling which all Universes use. A primary reality-frame or "Vault" is the Aeriopax, one of the Reshels' systems in the creation flow. The Eye of Ra can also be used as a Pillar (connective) supporting its Gate function. This Gate function uses two systems within the one Eye of Ra dynamic: two "Pillars of the Abode" which have between them the central pillar made up of a number of tubular templates including the Zoii (pure Life) central core, a Chorhii template and the "Layooesh" which has its own complex organization. Other templates would reflect the nature and objectives of the Form being supported the female to convert to conscious thought she perceives as "intuition." She then translates that to thought   forms and

and connected. (In Psalm 118:19-23 these systems are the Gates of Righteousness and the Gate of the Lord "into which the righteous shall enter.") The rhombic gate is also found in a "L" form as a format more convenient in temple and other grid construction.

From "Akashic Definitions" (www.spiritmythos.org): "The 'Eye of Ra' is the convergence point for this and many other universes. It is the 'Threshold'. The "outer membrane" is the actual "universal grid" (both half-light Oritoronic and full-light Metatronic) surrounding the Eye of Ra; containing the "worlds" such as Earth, that exist in the many universes."

MERKABAH: Hebrew word meaning "chariot." Modern application by mystics, defined by Thoth Raismes: "A vehicle or spirit-generated field of Light transport for sentient forms and consciousness through space and time." The ideal form, of many, would be the golden ratio rhombus system or "Eye of Ra" often correlating with the "L" geometric short method of forming a rhombus.

RANNA TIME FLOW: The complete hologram of Time as flows uninterrupted through the time-space dimensions of the Multi-Verse.

SHEKINAH: Hebrew meaning "dwelling place, resident of the dwelling place, abide, rest." The "rest" relates to the Unmanifest God (Void, Silence, Rest) as the source of life. This is vital in both male and female functions. Simply put: the male has no form but can inseminate any level of Form which is the female function and state of being. The Shekinah is the total female Presence or "Goddess"; She is the Generator that provides the Egg for initiating gestation and birth, ie the construction for all form including thought forms. She is the Manifested containment field and is often thought of as God's Cloak. She provides the male with his form. The male projects unformed fire codes as "knowing" to the female to convert to conscious matter. The wisdom gained in the process is returned to the male for him to reintegrated back into the flow of regeneration. Thus the male is constantly striving to become form (female) and the female to release the Form once generated.

In practical terms the total Female in the East is called the "Shakti" while in the Western Judeo-Christian format she is the "Sheeba" relating to the number 7 meaning the "whole." However "wholeness" is the complete female or Shekinah who requires the male for power and insemination. Thus he is found as the 8th aspect, often hidden. An example of basic duality is the female as John (Yahchanan) and the male as Jesus (Yeshua) in John 3:30 where Yeshua means "freedom, to call out" and Yahcanan means "Grace" with both names using the "Yud/Yah" as the significator. Yeshua "increases", that is, creates a product (female) ostensibly by calling out (vibration: sound and light). Yahchanan as the Shekinah uses the "chen" meaning Grace/love, to form a connective, to create form (a vineyard or foundation, a pedestal).

The Shekinah is also found in the name "Mari" relating to the Mar or Time continuum. Time is a function of thought forms, thus the female correlates with Time.. Most of Judeo-Christian scripture is a vast study of the Shekinah when the ostensibly male names are translated to reveal actual female functions and states of being.

SOLARIANS: The Solarians are those souls cultivated to be the guardians and servants of the Sacred Rays of Life Creation. The Solarians are in effect the scouts, the cosmic frontiersmen... those who clear the sacred Earth and raise the bridges and build the temples from the cosmic blueprint. There are also those souls with divine mission who are not from the Light Races of the "Children of the Sun" (Solarians) who have risen in later ages to assist. They, too, form circles of light on the Earth. Simply put, the Solarians represent the many stellar races, basically what we would relate to as "human", as compared to angelic or devic souls. Their programs would include generating avatars, messiahs, religions, nations and culture frames across Time. This is a large reason why safe and efficient Time gates are included in Light work: to collaborate with the Solarians and their projects in non-linear Time. Their symbols are the sacred birds (and the collective group of them), sometimes called the Starr-Eagles or Eagles of Starr. The Golden Bee is also their symbol. They have also been known as the Shepherds or Shepherd Kings.

STAR GATE: Stars are sentient beings of high order, they provide focal points in the Attasic Universe (all Universes) and generate the "Helio-Mar." A "Star Gate" can take many forms for specific functions but essentially it is a system that can bridge Matter and Anti-Matter in the dynamic universe forms while maintaining the real interface (bridge) point in the Neutra Universe having several creation templates: the foundational Selah (Unmanifest God: Life source), Grace/Love (beauty: divine harmonic of universal accord), and Mind. This unified field might also be called the "Chorhii", a nonpolarized state of being and knowing.

TELEPLANE: I have observed that light groups eventually expand to transcend linear time formats. They often see this continuum as a flat plane shimmering with a moon-light effect on ripples. Thus the archetype connects water with a time continuum. Also called a "vault, ark/arc, reality frame (as a 4-square)." Our 3-dimensional perception of reality is much like a holodeck in the Star Trek TV series. We are in a solid, Newtonian universe but projected as illusion from a flat plane (teleplane). The plane can be encoded into a straight line or staff/pillar or curve and sphere. The plane has two surfaces separated by a Selah Field or Void. This is divine Essence, ie the Unmanifest God. This is the basis of all reality frames. The ripple effect is apparently life force from the Void expressing as divine intelligence and as an objective quality of "Grace." Various systems have specific "gunas" or aspects of primal creation. Judeo Christian scriptures have many. The two sided mirror (Hebrew "mar") is a strong correlation with the nature of the teleplane.

ULTA POLE: This is the divine seed and system between the two planes of a continuum reality. It projects two clones of itself into the two planes that contain the Reshel's Shiyn poles. The Reshel grids generate from these planes to create the systems that support Metatronic creation.

Thoth/Maia says
"Between the two major guiding power realms is a point of balance called by the Inner Earth Illuminaries, the ULTA. The Ulta, in more scientific terms is known as the pyra-radical gate...the mechanism which encodes the pyra-conic Light frequencies (emitted by the 'Living Lights') into spectra color/ sonic bands. These bands are filtered down through the pyramid or spiral acting on and reacting with all levels of Integration until it reaches our human condition, at which point these bands are synchro-radiated to the bio-chronic field of the brain/mind complex. The pitch and meter of synthesis resulting from the matching of brain waves to the x-grams or program codes of Morphionic (divine) Light, determines the time ratio of our field of consciousness. What all of this essentially means is that the 'gate' controls our perception of reality and since 'reality' is nothing more than perception itself, the Ulta feeds us our reality in a frame of limited quanta release..."

Appendix A

Reshel Study Tours led by the author Jackie Queally
jac@celtictrails.co.uk

Jackie runs intensive Reshel study tours based in Roslin from time to time, and also there are occasional trips to other sites in areas of Norway and Scotland that link in with the early history of the Sinclairs and/or the Templars. In Rennes Le Chateau similar Reshel study sessions are offered, and it is hoped to run a similar study tour one day in Sintra in Portugal since the latter two sites energetically key into the Rosslyn matrix via various earth grids. Light work and experience of the Reshel is key to the Roslin tours. Details can be found at
www.templartrails.co.uk

Half and whole day and even longer personalised tours from Edinburgh operate all year round to Rosslyn Chapel and other key sites such as those on the Rose Line that William Buehler so named originally. These tours are flexible in content and include local legends and more general historical information unless clients request otherwise. Dowsing is an optional activity at the sites for instance.
www.celtictrails.co.uk

Appendix B

Contact Details
1. Rev, Maia Nartoomid has been an akashic channel for thirty nine years, Her Spirit Mythos website is extensive, containing much of her written work and Spirit Art. PDF files of her earlier writings are also available:
http://www.spiritmythos.org

2. William Buehler
roslinne@fairpoint.net

3. Rab Wilkie is a Perth-born anthropologist and astrologer now resident in Peterborough, Ontario.
Email: rab@peterboro.net; Website: www.astrocyclics.com

4. Aine Armour http://www.celticfireandfaerie.com/

Appendix C

Types of Grids by Bill Buehler
The geometric format *(example using the Tetrahedron and equilateral triangle)*
A simple triangle is an example of the Reshel, and it represents the "3" or CONNECTIVE function. It is efficient in communications, building a pillar or bridge. It has a high Grace Factor and its Master Number 666 is a Christic Temple Pillar (best described in Rev.3: verses 7-12 as the Pillar in the Temple of God: the letter Vau, 6, or Key of David.) The triangle or Key of David is poor for manifestation of form, its main form being a connective of forms. It is a pure symbol for a tetrahedron, that is the triangle usually showing the base and each of its sides projecting triangular flat planes into a single unifying apex over the base. An "altitude" line is dropped to the base at which point the tetrahedron's centre of power and action is designated, its "spiritual centre." The apex of the base triangle is the "pivot" and the other two sides are the right and left brain poles for the pivot pole.

For example, the primary spiritual mode orients the pivot pole in the north. The SE pole is the right brain pole for the system and the SW is the left brain pole. The northward or vertical ("up") pointing apices represent the female or *Shekinah* ascending vector. The opposite male, causal or Christic complement is formed when the female or physical system is brought into clarity and a harmonic with the Christic state of being. This then forms a dual or "star" tetrahedron made up of two interpenetrating tetrahedrons.

The other two main geometric systems are the SQUARE for MANIFESTING and the PENTAGON for a SEED MATRIX. Using the rationale above, the square or "+" Cross (Greek Cross) is complemented by the "X" Cross in which Spirit inserts its interface and codes when the physical cross is clear and up to speed. The same occurs with the 5-pointed star to give us a 10-pointed Wheel.

Every form then has a complete system of Seed, the Form and the Connective linking to the higher complementary Seed, Form and Connective. This is also the "Yahway" or "HVHY" creation Grid format.

2. A consciousness grid.

Of course all grids have consciousness. However again I am trying to indicate a grid without geometry and "random" does not fit the description. There is not a geometric form, usually, in this type of grid. The chakras are an example. The Planet has many grids that are formed of chakra sites, not geometrically organized. There can be chakras associated with geometric grids however this is not necessary all the time. A square can have chakras for example.

3. The zodiacal grid.

Often a zodiacal sign or portion of the sign will be used as a grid. The Templar Virgo Grid in Europe is a prime example, made up of the principal Marian cathedrals. It is usually more permanent. Most zodiacal grids are full systems

4. An Integral grid.

This system can be any of the others but is a basic structural grid without which the structure will collapse. A "skeleton" grid describes it. The Earth uses the geometric five Platonic Grids for example.

5. An Artifact grid.

This is an artificial system inserted for a specific purpose, usually a more permanent installation that is resonant with the others. A Zodiacal Grid is an Artifact however "artifact" here is used in a more general sense. An example is the Reshel system used in

Europe and the Americas. The Reshel or "Techad" supplements the total Planetary artifact grid: the Rhombic Enneacontahedron Grid made up of golden ratio rhombuses. (This RE grid was discovered by Marvin Solit.) The RE Grid complement the Platonic Grids, phasing with the Penta Dodecahedron and Icosahedron.

Appendix D

The 7/8 dynamic by Aine Armour-Barrett with introduction by William Buehler.

This note provides an excellent application of the "7."

I use the Number 7 as the whole, female dynamic. In the East the total female energy and state is called the "Shakti" but in the West, using Judeo Christian this would be the "Sheba" (7). The Book of Revelation uses quite a few 7-matrices, each with its context. With each there is the "8th" pole which is the male complement. (Most of the J-C scripture is given to defining the total female and her creational role. Her aspects are superficially hidden behind male and place names, one must translate the Hebrew to find the functions. Probably 80% of the J-C scriptures are devoted to female dynamics... NOT male as so many assume... never having taken the trouble to translate and interpret the evident systems.) In Revelation, for example, the 7 Churches are complemented by the 8th aspect: the Isle of Patmos.

Aine Armour-Barrett has come up with one of the finest applications of "7/8" I've seen for the modern mystic, in this Ascension phase: The number seven referred to above is the number of the female body/earth body. This body is the Kingdom of the Grail. It holds within it the seven gateways of Awakening

1. The physical earth body/nature/ visible outer form of the Kingdom of the Grail. The emotional feeling earth body/ centre of power for gathering information. The information gathered is on how the inner Goddess responds to (feels) the creational forces being used by the resident consciousness.

2. The power body protected by the Sword of Truth/ that which cuts through all illusion; the Sword protects the Heart Centre. Gateway to the Inner Realms.

3. The Heart Centre of LOVE. Centre of purification. Centre to Oneness. Holder of the codes of Sovereignty for the King.

4. The Sound Body. Doorway to the living Word – creational force/power behind and within all that is.

5. The Body of Vision. Gateway to Divine Seeing - the world of encoded light forms that fill of all creation. The ability to See the Light in all form.

6. The Body of Bliss and transcendence. The Stone of Sovereignty and Truth. The King holds the space for the healing of the Goddess/the body/the and/Shiva Shakti. Once the Body of Bliss is experienced within the Goddess (an experience of entering the Oneness/ the joining of the King and Goddess in the inner realm) she opens to the King in the outer World. The King is one who carries the codes but is not yet fully awakened. The awakening happens through his Service to the Goddess/ the Witnessing of her healing the WOUND. He becomes the Magnetic Floor of Safety (term from the Magdelen Manuscript) for her to release ALL imprints of the WOUND. When the WOUND is completely released from the body of 7 of the Goddess, it involves the releasing of the WOUNDED Grail King from suffering, if he so chooses. This is the awakening of the Triple Spiral and the 7 thus becomes the 777 gateway. When the King goes through the gateway of the 777 he is then prepared through a process of inner awakening to be the instrument for the insemination.

7. The insemination is the 8 before the act and the 888 after the Divine Union. All of Earth registers such a union through the Metatronic Grid. The Grid holds the frequency of this Divine

Union. This is the message from Ruta... The insemination brings all of creation between the King and the Goddess back into the Divine Harmonic. From such a union the Divine Child is born. When the mass of humanity enter this stage of Awakening the

Children thus born will be the foundation for the New World of Living Light - the Land of Sovereign Beings in conscious co-creation with Source.
Skellig Michael holds this frequency from Ruta. It is the 888 doorway to Alba On. Alba On is the gateway to all of Europe.

Aine Armour works consciously with the Old Tribe of Ireland, the Tuatha de Danann Sidhe. She gives workshops, private sessions and conducts sacred journeys to Ireland. She works with the Metatronic Grids and the Dragon Lines in the Earth. The group work in Ireland involves activations both for the participants and for the leys within the land. She is a poet, author and artist. For more details please see her site. http://www.celticfireandfaerie.com/

Appendix E
Skycharts Equinoctial Celestial Alignments At Rosslyn by Rab Wilkie

Skycharts for sunrise at the autumn equinox (St Matthew's Day) as seen from Rosslyn in AD 1446 and 2008.

Roslin: 55N52, 3W12
Equinox 2008: 22Sep GMT; sunrise: 5:59am GMT
Equinox 1446: 14Sep GMT; sunrise: 5:58am GMT
Direction: due East (90.0 azimuth)
Borthwick church: 111 degrees, (21 degrees south of East).

Celestial alignments of sacred sites and churches are not uncommon, especially among older churches which were by custom aligned to the rising sun on the calendar date of the day of the saint to which a church was dedicated, so there is nothing extraordinary about Rosslyn Chapel being oriented due east in the direction of sunrise at the equinoxes because the Day of St Matthew - the saint to which the Chapel was dedicated - was established by the Roman Church to coincide with the Spring Equinox. And since east-west alignments may be the most common anyway, irrespective of a church's dedication, Rosslyn's alignment may be thought of as perfectly prosaic. However, there are additional phenomena that make Rosslyn's situation unique.

At the March equinox three constellations rise with the Sun: Virgo, Leo, and Crater which are anciently associated with a divine Maiden or Goddess, the Lion/King, and a sacred Cup or Grail. Over time, the constellations associated with the equinox change, but for the last five hundred years or so they have shifted only a bit. Now, as in 1446 when the Chapel was built, the same three constellations rise with the Sun on Saint Matthews's Day.

These three adjacent constellations fill a triangular region of the sky with Leo uppermost and Crater south from Virgo - the constellation through which the Sun is passing on September 21st. But the Lion, which heralds the Sun's rise, can be 'couchant' or 'rampant' depending on latitude. Northward from Edinburgh, the Lion begins to lie down, and close to the equator he's almost falling over backwards, but within the latitudinal zone around 55 North his head is upright as he stands, much like it is on the Lion Rampant flag of Scotland.

At Rosslyn's latitude the Grail rises at the same moment as the Sun, but as we head further north the Grail rises later, and southward sooner. In 1446 the coordinated rise of Sun and Grail was much more precise.

Furthermore, the brightest star of Crater rises 21 degrees south of east, in line with Borthwick church, the Borthwicks having been cup-bearers to the Sinclairs.

Also in 1446, the Sun rose in conjunction with the star Porrima, named by the Romans after their ancient goddess of prophecy. The link here could be with the gospel of Matthew insofar as it's the astrological gospel - with the Christmas story and the coming of the Magi (astrologers) who saw "His star in the east".

The Sun now rises in Virgo, although no longer with Porrima. Instead, it now rises with Zavijava, made famous at the September equinox in 1922 when it was used to test Einstein's 'prophecy' about the speed of light. (He was right).

In 1446 on Saint Matthew's Day, Jupiter aligned with Denebola in Leo, the 'stand-in' star for our invisible or transcendent Sun, Mazuriel, on a higher plane of reality. Jupiter passes Denebola every twelve years, and often thrice within nine months, but even so, an equinoctial alignment is rare; and Jupiter is the planet of expansive, beneficent power and nobility – in this case amplified by the 'Sun behind the Sun', the spiritual source of true royalty.

Other phenomena which may provide clues to the current significance of Rosslyn:
Currently (1968-2044), sunrise at the September Equinox aligns with constellation Crater (Cup/Grail), located just below and on the back of the Water Snake (Hydra). Narrowing the timeframe to 2000-12, the Sun aligns with the bottom or pit of the Grail.

Also, Orion is due South, Betelgeuse and the figure's upraised hand exactly at 180 degrees azimuth. This is not surprising because that's the stellar geometry now. Orion and Auriga lies opposite the Galactic Centre. The stars of Orion's drawn Sword/Club and the four 'horses' of Auriga align precisely during 2000-2012 with the June Solstice.

Due North, and quite far above the horizon, is the red eye of the (Pen)Dragon, Eltanin. (The Pendragon's throat passes the zenith at the latitude of Roslin).

Due West, Uranus in Aquarius has just set, as it zigzags during the year back & forth across the cusp with Pisces, (the Aquarian Age cusp).

The Grail constellation is right below the Borthwick azimuth (111), and when the Sun, having risen, aligns with 111 at after 7am, the whole Grail has just appeared above the horizon further south.

Line of sight from Rosslyn relative to the altitude of the visual horizon, might reveal other alignments. Irrespective of time of year, Orion (Rigel & Saiph in particular), now rises in the 111 direction. When Rigel passes this azimuth, it is four degrees ($4^{20'}$) above the ideal horizon, and could be right on the real horizon.. depending on landscape & hills.

In summary, the Chapel's alignments, East & 111, appear to take both stars and planets into consideration, enabling the link between mundane astrology and transcendent or 'ascendant' light work - quite literally since sunrise on the September equinox includes Leo and the whole complex of Sun, Denebola/Mazuriel, and the Grail (plus 1446 Jupiter). In astrological terms, they are all 'on the Ascendant'.

The Grail Constellation lies just below the horizon at the 111 zone. At the latitude of Rosslyn, Denebola/Mazuriel currently passes due East after ideal sunrise and possibly at the time of equinoctial sunrise as seen on the horizon from Rosslyn. The

'Lyon' (Leo) has just risen - its tail, Denebola, having just cleared the horizon - as Crater (Grail)
clears the ideal horizon.

Leo and its brightest star, Regulus, are associated with royalty and the Lion flag of Scotland. In 2011-12 Regulus is the last bright zodiacal star to shift precessionally into its next zodiacal sign, in this case Virgo. Just a few centuries after the advent of the Piscean Age (70BC - AD70), such stars began moving out of their signs, and it will have taken almost 2000 years to complete the process.

From 2012, all constellations will have shifted one sign, in effect setting the stage for the union of The Lion & The Virgin.. but also The Scorpion & The Archer, The Grail Bearer and The Fish, and so on around the zodiac, uniting stellar/galactic and solar/terrestrial realms.

Rab Wilkie is a Perth-born anthropologist and astrologer now resident in Peterborough, Ontario.
Email: rab@peterboro.net;
Website: www.astrocyclics.com .

Appendix F: The Selah Bridge in the Brain.
(From THE SOURCE, #3-81, Thoth Raismes as translated by Rev. Maia Nartoomid)

"One of the most essential branches of Human/Earth sciences, and certainly one of the most complex, is 'geo-cerebral alignment'. This is the function of the brain in which it is attuned to a particular amplitude of the Earth's geo-dynamic register through the rotation of the cerebral matter of the brain within its liquid-cushioned cavity, to a 'critical rotational position' (CRP) in synch with a particular geo-register. From the centre of the Earth's inner sun is emanated a pulse which in turn is emitted as a frequency up and down the polar 'spine' of Earth-

--that polarized field between the poles, running through the planet.

"This frequency is radiated through the inner and outer ecospheres of Earth by the inner and outer resonant cavities. The inner resonant cavity (ecosphere of the hollow Earth) charges the surface crystalline grid of the planet, which interchanges frequencies with the outer resonant cavity between the Earth's surface and the ionosphere. The entire process brings about a holistic media of attunement through which all life becomes the sensor system of the planet. In order for biological species ---human, animal and vegetal to maintain the life-wave energies they must focus their neuro-sensors upon various frequency amplitudes on the geo-dynamic spectrum.

"This spectrum is a complex, computer-like scale registering codes or packages of cognitive directives created through the assimilation of various earth/solar/stellar processes. These code-packages are 'x-grams'. They are like energy programs for the Earth's ether computer printouts, giving the exact vibratory patterns of the many different parallaxes in which the neuro-activity of a brain/mind complex can align itself by cerebral rotation. The inner world inhabitants can, through a series of tonal frequencies and/or light patterns, command brain alignment to whatever geo-dynamic parallax chosen upon the spectrum.

"As an example: should there be presented to a subterranean physician a patient whose left arm was paralyzed as a result of an accident, the physician would treat the patient by submitting him to a tonal/optic computer which would locate the geo-dynamic parallax needed to restore the neural control of the left arm of this individual. Then, through tonal and/or optical stimulus the patient's CRP for that particular amplitude on the geo-dynamic scale would be activated. This treatment could almost certainly recover the complete use of the once paralyzed arm. However it is not as simple as it sounds. Were the programs or x-grams easy to decode our brain centres would be accidentally stimulated into major CRPs by a succession of honking horns or Beethoven's Fifth. In order to protect our brain/mind centres from violation of their own genetic response codes (which, when triggered fit like keys into the 'locks' of the x grams), the programs of the Earth's ether computer are complex and require intricate maneuvering of vibratory frequencies to elicit a major CRP.

"Minor CRPs are constantly being stimulated in our brain by sunlight, inaudible and audible sound waves, the motion of the Earth and other sense factions of our world. These minor or lesser CRPs are critical in the creation of our reality. The major or greater CRPs are intended to serve as major adjustments for our sensors when our bio-systems become radically out of step with the geo-dynamic spectrum in some respect. The activation of major CRPs perform much the same function as a circuit breaker's in recharging deactivated neuro-pulses and reestablishing the proper circadian rhythms erratically cycled neuro-pulses within our body's schematic. This process is also evidenced in the vegetal world.

"The CRPs of plants have been radionically detected. In 'The Secret Life of Plants' this movement is stated as: 'apparently established by the earth's magnetic field as the seed sprouts out of the ground (...If the seedling is transplanted in such a way that it continues to grow in its CRP it will thrive better than plants which have been transplanted out of that orientation) ...because of this apparent relationship with the geomagnetic field, a plant has a pattern of radiation around it. Node points within this pattern or web which seem to concentrate the field of radiation can be located by a portable detector with a probe and a rubbing plate similar to that on their radionics device.'

"Like plants, animals and humans also radiate a pattern about them. Through sophisticated plasma-based computers, inner terrestrial technicians can locate not only the node points within the pattern but their coded message, giving them the CRPs connected to the body's acupoints."